T0202992

SpringerBriefs in Computer Science

SpringerBriefs present concise summaries of cutting-edge research and practical applications across a wide spectrum of fields. Featuring compact volumes of 50 to 125 pages, the series covers a range of content from professional to academic. Typical topics might include:

- A timely report of state-of-the art analytical techniques
- A bridge between new research results, as published in journal articles, and a contextual literature review
- A snapshot of a hot or emerging topic
- An in-depth case study or clinical example
- A presentation of core concepts that students must understand in order to make independent contributions

Briefs allow authors to present their ideas and readers to absorb them with minimal time investment. Briefs will be published as part of Springer's eBook collection, with millions of users worldwide. In addition, Briefs will be available for individual print and electronic purchase. Briefs are characterized by fast, global electronic dissemination, standard publishing contracts, easy-to-use manuscript preparation and formatting guidelines, and expedited production schedules. We aim for publication 8-12 weeks after acceptance. Both solicited and unsolicited manuscripts are considered for publication in this series.

More information about this series at http://www.springer.com/series/10028

Grigori Sidorov

Syntactic n-grams
in Computational Linguistics

 Springer

Grigori Sidorov
Instituto Politécnico Nacional
Centro de Investigación en Computación
Mexico City, Mexico

ISSN 2191-5768   ISSN 2191-5776   (electronic)
SpringerBriefs in Computer Science
ISBN 978-3-030-14770-9   ISBN 978-3-030-14771-6   (eBook)
https://doi.org/10.1007/978-3-030-14771-6

Library of Congress Control Number: 2019935141

This Springer imprint is published by the registered company Springer Nature Switzerland AG
The registered company address is: Gewerbestrasse 11, 6330 Cham, Switzerland

Preface

This is a new substantially revised edition of the book, where we discuss the use of syntactic information (represented as syntactic n-grams) in the tasks of computational linguistics related to application of machine learning methods. We substantially revised and completed the book adding several new chapters.

The previous edition of this book was published several years ago in Spanish under the name of *Non-linear Construction of N-Grams in Computational Linguistics: Syntactic, Filtered, and Generalized N-Grams*, and we got very positive feedback from many researchers and students, who complimented us saying the book presents really novel idea, describes this idea in a very clear way, and besides presents the background in the very transparent manner, which makes it possible for many persons clarifying the procedures applied in the modern computational linguistics.

We made substantial changes in the book as compared to the previous edition adding several chapters, and we also added more examples in English. We also clarified the relationship between continuous and noncontinuous syntactic n-grams. Let us remind that the concept suggested in the book, syntactic n-grams, is a universal concept, which can be applied in any language.

We are delighted to present to the reader the modified book now in its English version.

This book is about a new approach in the field of computational linguistics related to the idea of constructing n-grams in a nonlinear manner, while the traditional approach consists in using the data from the surface structure of texts, i.e., the linear structure.

In this book, we propose and systematize the concept of syntactic n-grams, which allows using syntactic information within the automatic text processing methods related to classification or clustering. It is a very interesting example of application of linguistic information in the automatic (computational) methods. Roughly speaking, the suggestion is to follow syntactic trees and construct n-grams based on paths in these trees. There are several types of nonlinear n-grams; future work should determine which types of n-grams are more useful in which natural language processing (NLP) tasks. For clarification of the basic concept for the reader, we dedicate the first part of the book to explanation of basic concepts of computational linguistics and machine learning (vector space model, tf-idf, etc.) and explain the general scheme of design of the experiment in this field.

The book, first and foremost, is intended for specialists in the field of computational linguistics. However, we made an effort to explain in a clear manner how to use n-grams; we provide a large number of examples, and, therefore, we believe that the book is also useful for graduate students who already have some previous background in the field.

We want to emphasize that no profound knowledge of computing or mathematics is required; the proposed concepts are intuitively very clear; we use very few formulas, and if they appear, they are explained in detail.

Mexico City, Mexico   Grigori Sidorov

Introduction

In this book, we discuss a novel idea in the field of computational linguistics: the construction of n-grams in a nonlinear manner.

First, we discuss the concept of the vector space model in detail – a conceptual framework for comparison of any type of objects and then its application to the text processing-related tasks, i.e., its use in computational linguistics. Concepts related to word frequency (*tf-idf*) are discussed, and the latent semantic analysis that allows reducing the number of dimensions is briefly presented.

We mention important concepts concerning the design of experiments in computational linguistics and describe the typical scheme of experiment in this area.

We present the concept of traditional (linear) n-grams and compare it with the concept of n-grams obtained in a nonlinear manner: syntactic, filtered, and generalized n-grams.

Syntactic n-grams are n-grams constructed by following paths in syntactic trees. The great advantage of syntactic n-grams is that they allow introducing pure linguistic (syntactic) information into machine learning methods. The disadvantage is that syntactic parsing is required for their construction (note that already there are syntactic parsers available for many languages).

We consider both continuous and noncontinuous syntactic n-grams. When constructing continuous syntactic n-grams, bifurcations (returns, interruptions, ramification) in the syntactic paths are not allowed; when removing this constraint, noncontinuous syntactic n-grams are obtained: sub-trees of length n with bifurcations of a syntax tree are considered. It is noteworthy that we can unite these two types of sn-grams: continuous and noncontinuous syntactic n-grams are complete syntactic n-grams; it is all sub-trees of length n.

We propose a metalanguage for the representation of noncontinuous syntactic n-grams, i.e., a formal way to represent a noncontinuous syntactic n-gram using brackets and commas, e.g., "a b [c [d, e], f]." In this case, brackets and commas are a part of the sn-grams.

In this book, we also present several examples of construction of continuous and noncontinuous syntactic n-grams for syntactic trees obtained using the FreeLing and the Stanford parsers.

We show that the application of syntactic n-grams in one of the traditional computational linguistics tasks, the task of authorship attribution, gives better results than using traditional n-grams.

Finally, we present several ideas concerning the other types of nonlinearly constructed n-grams:

1. Filtered n-grams: a filter of words or features is built using a certain criterion before constructing n-grams; then n-grams are constructed using only the elements that passed through the filter.
2. Generalized n-grams: words "are generalized" using lexical relations, especially synonymy and hypernymy; in this way, the set of elements used for constructing n-grams is reduced.

Many experimental studies are required in order to determine which construction parameters of continuous and noncontinuous, filtered, and generalized n-grams are the best and for which existing tasks in computational linguistics.

The book systematizes the recent author's proposals on the nonlinear construction of n-grams and their use in vector space model; thereby, some parts of the book are based on the author's previous works published in various journals and conferences with updates and necessary adjustments.

Work is done under the partial support of the Mexican government (CONACYT, SNI); Mexico City government (ICYT-DF PICCO10-120 project); National Polytechnic Institute, Mexico (projects SIP, COFAA); CONACYT project 240844; and FP7 PEOPLE-2010 IRSES: Web Information Quality Evaluation Initiative (WIQ-EI) European Commission project 269180.

Contents

Part I
Vector Space Model in the Analysis
of Similarity between Texts

Chapter 1
Formalization in Computational Linguistics

1.1 Computational Linguistics

Computational linguistics is an important area within the field of linguistics. Computational methods used in computational linguistics originate from computer science, or, to be more specific, from artificial intelligence. However, the primary object of study of computational linguistics remains the modeling of human language, and therefore it continues to be a part of the field of humanities.

Computational linguistics studies how to construct language models so as to be understandable by the computers; that means that it not only analyzes the use of language in human behavior but also applies specific formal methods that allow the exact formulation of the hypotheses and their subsequent automatic evaluation using linguistic data (corpora) [32, 51, 66].

1.2 Computational Linguistics and Artificial Intelligence

The formal part of computational linguistics is related to the methods of artificial intelligence [49]. In general terms, we can define the purpose of the science of artificial intelligence as formal modeling of human intelligence; i.e., the questions that artificial intelligence answers are: What is intelligent behavior? How do humans solve so many practical problems on a daily basis, in most cases without committing errors? Not all areas of artificial intelligence are related to human language, for example, vision or problem solving, etc. However, in artificial intelligence, several methods applicable to any type of data have been developed: methods of machine learning; precisely these methods are applied in modern computational linguistics turning it into a formalized science. To some extent, computational linguistics becomes an empirical science, where hypotheses are verified based on the experiments.

G. Sidorov, *Syntactic n-grams in Computational Linguistics*, SpringerBriefs
in Computer Science, https://doi.org/10.1007/978-3-030-14771-6_1

1.3 Formalization in Computational Linguistics

Computers are the most important modern tools that have ever been created by mankind. However, the nature of computers is a simple binary logic: zeros, ones, and some logical operations upon them. How to transform such a complex phenomenon as human language into this simple logic? For this reason, computational linguistics uses both the knowledge we have about the human language and the existing tools in the area of computer science and mathematics: various types of formal models, programming languages, etc. [11].

Indeed, it is curious that many modern studies in the field of computational linguistics increasingly resemble other areas of computer science and artificial intelligence, especially machine learning-related areas: automatic classification or automatic clustering. Nevertheless, we insist that without the linguistic part, these methods cannot be applied in human language models. In this case, the part related to linguistics consists in selecting the features (and their values) that are introduced into the classification and clustering algorithms. So why the step toward the use of formal methods was taken precisely in recent years? From our point of view, this is related to the advances of the Internet where a large number of texts are freely available these days. These texts are an excellent source for learning of the automatic systems. Although it seems that modern automatic systems can do magic – to take data and perform tasks so much like a human being – in fact, they are based on the application of machine learning methods to exceedingly big data sets.

The most common and probably the only way to apply machine learning methods is to use the vector space model. Obviously, it is one of the most commonly used models in modern computational linguistics. The following chapters briefly explain this concept and discuss possible values that can be represented in vector space in case of texts.

Chapter 2
Vector Space Model

2.1 The Main Idea of the Vector Space Model

First of all, everything that will be explained below is very simple and does not require any computational knowledge, rather only a common sense. Therefore, we suggest the reader to continue without the fear of encountering profound mathematics; we try to explain the few formulas that appear here as clearly as possible.

The vector space model is a widely used model in computer science. Its wide use is due to the simplicity of the model and its very clear conceptual basis that corresponds to the human intuition in processing information and data. The idea behind the model is very simple, and it is an answer to the question, how can we compare objects in a formal way? It seems that the only way to describe the objects is to use a representation with features (characteristics) and their values. It is a universal idea, and it even seems to be the only possible way to work with formal objects [96].

Perhaps, the other option could be the use of associative memories [49]; in this case, instead of the features and their values, the relations between the objects are used; the relations are expressed through artificial neurons with corresponding connections; the connections have the corresponding weights. There is a large amount of literature on this subject; however, we will not discuss it in this book.

Well, now we know how to represent two (or more) objects by selecting the features and their values. Note that, in this case, to select the features means to build a model of our objects. Thus, the selection of the features is subjective, but the subsequent comparison is already completely objective.

It is necessary to mention that the selection of the values scale for the features also affects the model we are building, and this is a decision to be made, for example, it is not the same to measure in grams or in tons.

© The Author(s), under exclusive license to Springer Nature Switzerland AG 2019
G. Sidorov, *Syntactic n-grams in Computational Linguistics*, SpringerBriefs
in Computer Science, https://doi.org/10.1007/978-3-030-14771-6_2

2.2   Example of the Vector Space Model

To get a clear picture, let us provide an example. Suppose we want to compare two books. Which features shall we select? As mentioned above, it to a great extent depends on our needs, i.e., there is no unique and correct set of the objects features. However, some features are more common than others, for example, in the case of books, the "number of pages" would be an important feature for many purposes. There could also be such features as "cover color," "author," "publisher," "sociological profile" of the people who liked this book, etc.

The value of the "number of pages" feature would be numeric, i.e., it would be represented by a number. For the "publisher," the values would be a list of possible publishers. For the feature "sociological profiles," the values would be a little harder to represent, for example, "undergraduate students of the first year" or "university professors between 40 and 50 years old," etc. We stress once again that the selection of both features and their values is our own choice, i.e., we are the ones who are building the model, and it would be a matter of its practical application to see whether it is useful or not. This idea is very clear in the case of features; moreover, it is often applied to values. For example, we can measure the weight in kilograms or grams – this decision will greatly affect the subsequent comparisons between objects.

Now we have the representation of two objects in terms of features and their values. What is the next step? What else is needed to build a vector space model? Should it be something very complex? Certainly not, in fact, the model is already built. It is a space of N dimensions; each dimension in this space corresponds to a feature: the number of dimensions is equal to the number of features of the object in our model.

One can imagine a dimension as an axis in which we can mark the values of a feature/dimension. If the values are numeric, the interpretation is clear – it is the distance from the point with coordinates $(0,0,\ldots)$. If the values are naturally ordered, for example, age ranges, it is also clear how to treat them, although we have to assign them some numerical values. If the values are not related, for example, the cover color of a book, the easiest solution is to use a random order and equally assign numerical values to each symbolic value.

Note that if we want to handle this situation properly, we can introduce as many new dimensions (features) as many values we have for each feature, and their values can be "present-absent" (1 or 0). The advantage is that, in this case, we do not have to sort the values; the drawback is that the number of dimensions significantly increases. In neural networks, this encoing is called "one hot" encoding.

The next step is related to the following questions: Where the vectors are and why is it a vector space? As already mentioned, each object is a set of features and their values, which corresponds to exactly one point in a space of N dimensions (the dimensions correspond to the features). This point corresponds to a vector (an arrow in the geometric representation) of N dimensions (n-dimensional vector), which starts at the point with the coordinates $(0,0,0,\ldots)$ in this space. For example, let's consider a 100 page book with *red* cover and compare it with a 50 page book with *green* cover. This is a two-dimensional space, "number of pages" and "cover color," and each book is a point with coordinates [100, *red*] and [50, *green*]. Note that we have to choose which numerical values correspond to *red* and *green*.

The dimensions correspond to the position of the particular values in the vector, i.e., feature number 1 has the position 1 in the vector, feature number 2 has the position 2, etc. In this case, as all dimensions are equal, the ordering of the features never affects the model.

Another question is how can we formally represent the vector spaces? As already mentioned, each object is a set of values of the selected features, for example, one book is presented as $X = [(number\ of\ pages = 100), (cover\ color = red)]$ and the other one as $Y = [(number\ of\ pages = 50), (cover\ color = green)]$. Two questions arise: (1) Is there a need to repeat each time the name of the feature? and (2) What can be done if an object does not have any value of a given feature?

The answer to the first question is simple, the feature name is usually omitted, thus $X = [100, red]$ and $Y = [50, green]$. Recall that the value of the same feature has the same index in the vector, i.e., the same position in the vector. Another explanation can be based on a table where the columns correspond to the objects and the rows to the features (or it can be the other way around, it does not change the model), see Table 2.1. In this regard, tabular representation (matrix) and vector representation are the same: the columns correspond to the objects and the rows to the features, while the value of each cell is the value of the feature of a given object.

In this sense, the mere fact of knowing the column of the value already defines to which feature this value corresponds, i.e., this kind of information is directly known from its position in a table.

The answer to the second question is equally simple, what is to be done if a feature is simply not defined for a given object: the corresponding positions are filled in with zero values. In all subsequent calculations, these values will not affect the result being equal to zero.

Note that the tabular representation is conceptually the same as the vector space model per se: the columns correspond to the dimensions. The only difference is that, in this case, it is not so natural to use geometric concepts that we present below, but the advantage of this representation is that later we can apply the methods of linear algebra, e.g., the latent semantic analysis (LSA). We will provide an example of application of these methods below.

Table 2.1 Example of the vector space tabular representation

	Book X	**Book** Y
Dimension 1: *Number of pages*	*100*	*50*
Dimension 2: *Cover color*	*Red*	*Green*

2.3 Similarity of Objects in the Vector Space Model

What are the advantages of the vector space concept? We have already built it, how does it help us? It turns out that we can use the metaphor of space to calculate the similarity between objects, i.e., to compare objects based only on very simple geometrical notions, not more complicated than the Pythagorean theorem as explained below.

Now, each object is a vector in a space of N dimensions. How can we compare these vectors? The geometric principle states that the vectors in more or less the same direction resemble each other. Formally speaking, the more acute the angle between the vectors, the greater the similarity. It is very clear and intuitive in a two-dimensional space. For example, in Fig. 2.1, the more acute the angle between each pair of arrows, the more "similar" the arrows of this pair, i.e., their directions most closely coincide.

For example, vectors A and B resemble each other more than vectors B and C. And of course vectors A and C are least similar to one another. Note that when having three vectors, we can compare three pairs of vectors in total.

In a space with a larger number of dimensions, it is harder to imagine this similarity; therefore, we always suggest considering examples in a two-dimensional space taking into account that in a space with a larger number of dimensions, the principles would be exactly the same.

2.4 Cosine Similarity Between Vectors

In order to formally express the similarity, we use the cosine measure of the angle between vectors: the more acute the angle, the greater the cosine, i.e., the greater the similarity between vectors, and thus, the compared objects are more similar.

To calculate the cosine similarity between two vectors V and U, the inner product (dot product) of the normalized vectors is used. The normalization consists in dividing the result by the length of each vector or, equivalently, in multiplying their lengths. The length is called the Euclidean norm and is denoted, for example, by $\|V\|$ for the vector V.

Fig. 2.1 Example of the vector space: similarity between vectors

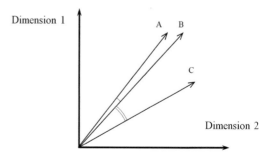

We would like to remind the reader what is "to normalize" and why it is important. Often it is crucial not to compare absolute values, but relative ones. For example, is 10 greater or less than 20? The question seems to make no sense, because obviously 20 is greater than 10. However, what if we knew that 10 was in the range of 30, and 20 was in the range of 100? In this case, if we normalize these values: 10/30 is greater than 20/100. This demonstrates that if the scale is taken into account (the same scale is used) when comparing values, the results depend on the normalization (scale). In the case of two-dimensional vectors, one vector can be a very long arrow while the other a short arrow. In order to be able to compare their similarity, we have to convert them into unit vectors using the Euclidean norm.

The dot product of two vectors is a value that is easy to obtain: Multiplications of the vector values in each dimension are summed up. In two dimensions (dimension 1 and dimension 2), for vectors U and V, it would be:

$$\text{Dot\_product}\left(V,U\right) = V_1 \times U_1 + V_2 \times U_2.$$

That is, the first elements of the vectors are multiplied among themselves and then the same with the second elements of the vectors, and at the end, the products are summed up.

More generally:

$$\text{Dot\_product}\left(V,U\right) = \sum_{n=1}^{m}\left(V_n \times U_n\right),$$

where m is the number of dimensions in the vector space model (which is equal to the vectors' length).

As already mentioned, the normalization of the vectors is the second step in the calculation of the cosine (the first is the calculation of the dot product). To this end, the length of the vectors is to be calculated, and the Euclidean norm is to be obtained. The Euclidean norm converts each vector into a unit vector (a vector of length 1). The normalization using the Euclidean norm $\|V\|$ is the division of the vector by its length. The vector length is calculated as follows:

$$\|V\| = \sqrt{\sum_{k=1}^{m}V_k^2}.$$

In the case of two dimensions, this corresponds to the application of the Pythagorean theorem:

$$\|V\| = \sqrt{V_1^2 + V_2^2},$$

where V_1 and V_2 are the values of the vector V on the axis 1 and 2. Actually, V_1 is the value of the vector in the dimension 1, i.e., the length of the first leg, and V_2 is the value of the vector in the dimension 2, i.e., the length of the second leg; see Fig. 2.1. In this case, the vector itself corresponds to the hypotenuse, and the Pythagorean theorem is applied.

In the case of a larger number of dimensions, the corresponding elements are added to the formula in the same way.

Thus, the final formula[1] for calculating the cosine similarity consists in obtaining the dot product of two vectors and applying the Euclidean norm:

$$\text{sim}(V,U) = \frac{\sum_{n=1}^{m} (V_n \times U_n)}{\|V\| \times \|U\|}.$$

In this case, the cosine similarity indicates to which extent the vectors V and U are similar. For positive values, the cosine ranges between 0 and 1.

Note that the cosine similarity is defined for exactly two objects (two vectors). The similarity of an object with itself would be equal to 1. For objects that correspond to the orthogonal vectors (i.e., the angle between them is 90°), the cosine similarity is equal to 0.

The concepts presented in this chapter are quite simple; nevertheless, they allow comparing any type of objects using (1) the vector space model, (2) the corresponding spatial metaphor, and (3) basic geometrical notions.

---

[1] Translator's remark: Note that this measure was generalized into soft cosine measure by Sidorov et al. [95], when the similarity of features is taken into account; see also Wikipedia.

Chapter 3
Vector Space Model for Texts and the *tf-idf* Measure

3.1 Features for Text Represented in Vector Space Model

Now we know what a vector space model for any type of objects is. This model consists in selection of features and assignment of values to these features, which allows to represent our objects as vectors and then to measure their similarity applying the cosine similarity formula. Recall that for the similarity calculation, exactly two objects have to be considered; in the case of a larger number of objects, the similarity (comparisons between objects) is calculated in pairs.

Let's see how this model is applied for the comparison of documents (texts). That is, the objects that we want to compare are documents.

The need for measuring similarity is a very typical situation in automatic natural language processing and computational linguistics tasks. For instance, the most common information retrieval task is precisely the calculation of similarity. We will explain it in a little more detail.

Information retrieval is based on a collection of documents; this collection can be quite large. In the case of the Internet search engines, this collection consists of all the Internet texts previously indexed by the "spiders," i.e., the programs that follow the links on the Internet (the World Wide Web). A user makes a query which also has a textual form. In this case, the retrieval task is to find the documents in the collection which to a larger extent "look like" the query, i.e., they are similar to the query [7]. As additional criterion, other criteria of similarity such as user profiles or the collection structure (e.g., as in the *PageRank* algorithm) are often used.

Now, if we want to compare the documents and the suggested way is to use the vector space model, how do we select the documents features? What are the features and their values? As always with the vector space model, we have many options, and it is up to us which features we will consider important and how we will select their values. Thus, in the vector space model, the comparison is objective, but the selection of the features and their values is subjective.

© The Author(s), under exclusive license to Springer Nature Switzerland AG 2019   11
G. Sidorov, *Syntactic n-grams in Computational Linguistics*, SpringerBriefs
in Computer Science, https://doi.org/10.1007/978-3-030-14771-6_3

The simplest way is to use words as documents features. Usually some additional procedures are implemented, such as lemmatization, i.e., all word forms are replaced by their lemmas. For example, the normalized forms *worked*, *working*, etc. correspond to the lemma *work*. Furthermore, the similarity calculation often excludes auxiliary words (stop words) such as prepositions or articles, since their presence in a document bears no information on the document itself, but determined by the characteristics of the language. It is common for many tasks; however, there are specific tasks which require the presence of such words, for example, authorship identification [4].

3.2   Values of Text Features: *tf-idf*

If words are used as features, what values may they have? Intuitively, the values should be somehow related to word frequency. In this sense, the more frequent the word, the more important is this word for a document. Not everything is that simple, but this is the main point.

The frequency of the word in a text document is called *tf* (term frequency), i.e., word (term) frequency shows how many times the word appears in a document. More specifically, it is denoted by tf_{ij}, i.e., how many times the word i appears in the document j. In this sense, it is a value that may differ for each document in the collection.

Normally the frequency of a word is combined with another measure, called *idf* (inverse document frequency). The intuition behind the *idf* is related to the following: if a word appears in all the documents of our collection, then this word cannot distinguish between these documents, and therefore is not useful. Conversely, if a word appears only in one document of our collection, it is a very useful word for similarity calculation (or, for example, for information retrieval which, as already mentioned, is a particular case of similarity calculation). The *idf* is calculated for each word in a given collection, i.e., it depends on the collection but does not depend on a specific document in the collection.

The formula for calculating the *idf* is the following:

$$idf_i = \log \frac{N}{\mathrm{DF}_i},$$

where N is the total number of documents in the collection, DF_i is the number of documents where the word i appears at least once, i.e., in this case, no matter how frequent the word is within the document, if it appears only once, it is already sufficient; note that this convention is verified by practice.

It can be observed that if a word appears in all the documents, then the value of the *idf* is equal to log(N/N), which is equal to 0. The *idf* value is the highest when a word appears in only one document (log($N/1$)).

The logarithm is used to soften the influence of the high frequencies; it is a typical use of logarithms in computational linguistics. Note that DF_i can never be equal to zero, because we have considered only the words that are present in our collection. Instead of *tf* we may also use its logarithm: $\log(tf + 1)$. In this case, we have to anticipate the possibility of zero, so we use "+1."

In general case, it is recommended to combine *tf* and *idf* of a given word for each document: normally they are multiplied. The measure that combines these two metrics is called *tf-idf*, and it is often used as the value of features in the vector space model for the documents comparison. One can apply not only *tf-idf* but also pure *tf*, normalized *tf*, *idf*, etc. [51].

3.3 Term-Document Matrix

So, the objects we are considering are documents (texts). Words (terms) are features of these documents; each word has a *tf-idf* value for each document. That means that each document corresponds to a vector of *tf-idf* values of words.

We can also represent all this information as a matrix. This matrix is called "term-document matrix." An example is presented in Fig. 3.1.

The documents $Doc_1...Doc_N$ represent the documents in our collection, the words $Word_1...Word_M$ represent all the words that appear in these documents; the words are ordered in a specific way. The values in the table correspond to the assumed *tf-idf* values in the collection.

Note that the table is usually highly sparse, i.e., it contains many zeros. Therefore, it is recommended to use the inverted index for its representation. The inverted index consists in converting the table into a list. For example, the inverted list for the figure above would be:

$(Doc_1, Word_1, 0.3), (Doc_1, Word_2, 0.7), (Doc_1, Word_5, 1.2), (Doc_2, Word_2, 0.01),$
$(Doc_3, Word_4, 2.2), (Doc_4, Word_1, 0.02), (Doc_4, Word_2, 0.5).$

Fig. 3.1 Term-document matrix

	Doc_1	Doc_2	Doc_3	Doc_4
$Word_1$	0.3	0	0	0.02
$Word_2$	0.7	0.01	0	0.5
$Word_3$	0	0	0	0
$Word_4$	0	0	2.2	0
$Word_5$	1.2	0	0	0
...				

In this case, there is no need to keep any elements for the zero values in the list. The initial matrix and the inverted index contain the same information. It is a standard procedure that should always be applied to sparse matrices.

It can be noted that this representation is equal to the vector representation, for example, the document Doc_1, as shown in Fig. 3.1, corresponds to the vector [0.3, 0.7, 0, 0, 1.2].

We will use the matrix (tabular) representation when discussing the latent semantic analysis.

3.4 Traditional n-grams as Features in Vector Space Model

Note that when using words as features, the information about the syntactic relations between the words is lost. The words become what is called "bag of words." However, for many tasks this loss of information is acceptable. Later in the book, we will propose a possible solution to avoid this loss of syntactic information: syntactic n-grams.

What else, apart from the words, could be the features of documents? Perhaps, it is hard to come up with it fast from scratch, but the concept itself is very simple; it refers to (traditional) n-grams. The simplicity of the described models is something that we have already mentioned when talking about the vector space model, and we believe that we are convincing the reader that it is actually so.

Traditional n-grams are sequences of elements as they appear in a document [66]. In this case, the letter n indicates how many elements have to be taken into account, i.e., the length of a sequence or of an n-gram. For example, there are bigrams (2-grams), trigrams (3-grams), 4-grams, 5-grams, and so on. Thus, if we talk about unigrams, i.e., n-grams constructed of a single element, it is the same as talking about words.

There are different types of elements that form n-grams. These elements can be lemmas or words; they can also be part of speech tags (POS tags) such as nouns, verbs, etc. The tags can be more detailed, i.e., include grammatical features, for example, a label VIP1S could mean "verb, indicative, present, first person, singular." We can construct n-grams using this kind of tags.

In recent years, character n-grams (character sequences taken from a text) are being used in various different tasks. Interestingly, for some tasks, such as authorship attribution, character n-grams give fairly good results [102]. Their linguistic interpretation is not sufficiently clear and remains an open question.

Let's see an example of traditional n-grams of words. For the sentence *John reads an interesting book*, we can obtain the following bigrams (2-grams): *John reads, reads an, an interesting, interesting book*. Or the following trigrams (3-grams): *John reads an, reads an interesting, an interesting book*, etc. We can replace each word for its lemma or part of speech and construct the corresponding n-grams. As we can see, the process is very simple, but it is successfully used in the computational linguistic systems.

If n-grams are used as features, what values may they have? As in the case of words (unigrams), these are the values related to their *tf-idf*. Note that the frequencies of n-grams are usually much lower than the frequencies of words, i.e., n-grams appear much less in a text. It is logical since we actually observe the appearance of sequences of two or more words together, which is a much less likely event than a single word.

Thus, in order to apply the vector space model to texts, we can use n-grams as features. These n-grams can be of various sizes, composed of elements of various types, and their values can be frequencies of *tf*, *idf*, or *tf-idf*.

Chapter 4
Latent Semantic Analysis (LSA): Reduction of Dimensions

4.1 Idea of the Latent Semantic Analysis

After building the vector space model, we can represent and compare any type of objects of our study. Now we can discuss the question whether we can improve the vector space we have built. The importance of this question is related to the fact that the vector space model can have thousands of features, and possibly many of these features are redundant. Is there any way to get rid of the features that are not that important?

There are several methods of analysis of the dependencies between features, for example, principal component analysis (PCA), the correlation coefficient, etc. In this chapter, we will briefly describe the method that is called latent semantic analysis (LSA) or latent semantic indexing (LSI) [18].

First of all, there is a need to clarify that although the idea of the latent semantic analysis applied to texts is to find the words that behave similarly (based on the analysis of their contexts) and, in this sense, have the same semantics, in most cases, the results have nothing to do with semantics, except for the initial intention. That is, the idea is to search for the semantic distributional similarity; however, in practice, this similarity is very hard to find applying the latent semantic analysis.

In fact, the latent semantic analysis is an application of a matrices processing technique taken from linear algebra. This technique is called singular value decomposition (SVD) and allows finding the rows with more information (large values) in the matrices and thereby eliminates the rows with less information (small values).

In this sense, for our purposes, the latent semantic analysis is just a technique to reduce dimensions of a vector space. Well, and why are we suddenly talking about matrices? And how the matrices are related to the dimensions? We have already discussed this issue in the section related to the term-document matrix: the objects are represented as vectors – this corresponds to a multidimensional space, but the set of vectors represents a matrix.

4.2   Examples of the Application of the Latent Semantic Analysis

In this book, we will not enter into mathematical details of the latent semantic analysis. Instead, we will provide a couple of simple examples. The intuition behind the latent semantic analysis can be represented in two ways.

Let us consider a matrix that characterizes four objects: O_1 to O_4, and uses four features: f_1 to f_4. It can be seen that the values of each pair of features are repeated. In this sense, one feature in each pair is redundant, see Fig. 4.1.

Suppose we apply the latent semantic analysis to these data. We have to indicate the desired number of dimensions at the output; in our case, we know that the number of dimensions is two (two features).

Note that the number of objects remains unchanged, i.e., equal to four. The values corresponding to each feature and each object were changed; however, the four objects we have are well described by the two new features, and the elimination of the two other features did not affect their descriptive capacity.

In another example, we consider two dimensions, in each of which a value is marked. We can map these two dimensions to another dimension, as shown in Fig. 4.2. The projections in the new dimension describe our objects just the same.

We can use another metaphor to describe the latent semantic analysis. It consists in the rotation of our multidimensional space to keep our data with minor changes as possible, and, at the same time, get rid of some dimensions.

	O_1	O_2	O_3	O_4
c_1	1	1	0	0
c_2	1	1	0	0
c_3	0	0	1	1
c_4	0	0	1	1

$\Rightarrow$ LSA

	O_1	O_2	O_3	O_4
$c_1{}'$	−1.4	−1.4	0	0
$c_3{}'$	0	0	−1.4	−1.4

Fig. 4.1 Example of the application of the LSA

Fig. 4.2 Projections to a new dimension

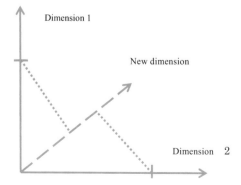

4.3 Usage of the Latent Semantic Analysis

As mentioned above, the latent semantic analysis is a way to reduce dimensions in a vector space model. It is considered that the latent semantic analysis reflects the distributional properties of its elements, i.e., allows capturing the contexts similarity of words or n-grams; however, in practice, it is hard to present clear cases.

When applying the latent semantic analysis, it is important to indicate the following parameter: how many dimensions should be in the new vector space, i.e., how many dimensions should be reduced. It is recommended to try values between 100 and 500 dimensions, although it is to be verified experimentally for each task.

There are libraries that implement the latent semantic analysis; therefore, we recommend using a freely available code (C, Python, etc.). The latent semantic analysis is a procedure that consumes some computational processing time; however, this procedure is not excessively long.

Chapter 5
Design of Experiments in Computational Linguistics

5.1 Machine Learning in Computational Linguistics

As we mentioned earlier in the book, in the automatic analysis of natural language (natural language processing, NLP) and in computational linguistics, machine learning methods are becoming more and more popular. Applying these methods increasingly gives better results [30, 35, 37, 41, 51, 72, 76, 84, 87, 100, 101].

The main purpose of applying the machine learning methods is to try to model the hypotheses formulated by linguists and its further evaluation. In this case, human intuition is replaced by large amounts of textual data – possibly with additional labels made manually – and by sophisticated learning methods based on mathematics and statistics. The intension is not to replace the linguists in the research process but to develop tools that can be useful for them.

Furthermore, the application of the machine learning methods allows an accurate evaluation of the language hypotheses and the reproduction of the results and, to some extent, makes computational linguistics a more exact science. In this sense, some branches of computational linguistics already require empirical procedures when the formulated hypothesis is verified using computational experiments based on the data, and not only on the intuition of native speakers or the experimenter himself.

In the modern computational linguistics, the supervised machine learning methods are the most commonly used, i.e., manually labelled data is used for training. Another option is related to the use of the unsupervised methods, when the system itself has to learn directly from the data. Of course, it is much more complicated to use the unsupervised methods, because in this case, the computer itself has to analyze the data without any human intervention. Normally a huge amount of data is needed to be able to apply these methods.

In computational linguistics, the most used specific machine learning methods are Naive Bayes (NB), support vector machines (SVM), and classifier based on decision trees (J48).

G. Sidorov, *Syntactic n-grams in Computational Linguistics*, SpringerBriefs in Computer Science, https://doi.org/10.1007/978-3-030-14771-6_5

5.2 Basic Concepts in the Design of Experiments

As mentioned above, in computational linguistics, common concepts of information retrieval can be applied [7] – precision and recall, which measure the viability of a hypothesis in a formal way. The harmonic mean of these two measures is called $F1$ measure. We always recommend using the latter for the comparison of methods. These are relatively simple concepts. Assume that we have a collection of documents, a query, and a system that we are evaluating. The system generates an output, i.e., presents some retrieved documents which the system considers relevant for the query; we will call them "all retrieved."

Among these documents, some are retrieved correctly, i.e., these are relevant documents: "relevant, retrieved." While others are retrieval errors committed by the system – these are "not relevant, retrieved" documents. That means that the set we call "all retrieved" consists of "relevant, retrieved" and "not relevant, retrieved" documents.

Hence the concept of precision emerges: How good is the answer with respect to itself? How many documents in the output are correctly retrieved? Precision (P) is the ratio of the "relevant, retrieved" documents to all retrieved documents ("all retrieved").

$$P = \frac{\text{relevant, retrieved}}{\text{all retrieved}}.$$

For example, the precision is 1 when all the documents in the output are correctly retrieved.

There can be, however, other documents relevant to the query, which the system did not manage to retrieve, let's call them "relevant, not retrieved." Hence the concept of recall (R) emerges: How good (specific) was the output of the system with respect to the collection? Were we able to retrieve most of the relevant documents or only a few? Thus, recall is the ratio of the "relevant, retrieved" to all relevant documents ("all relevant"); the latter set includes "relevant, retrieved" and "relevant, not retrieved" documents.

$$R = \frac{\text{relevant, retrieved}}{\text{all relevant}}.$$

Recall equals 1 when the system retrieves all the relevant documents. There is always a relation between precision and recall: if we try to increase one of those values, the other decreases.

Finally, the formula for the $F1$ measure that combines precision P and recall R is:

$$F1 = \frac{2 \times P \times R}{P + R}.$$

The measure is called $F1$ because the same weights are assigned to the precision and recall, which are equal to 1. In the case of assigning different weights, we can have $F2$ or $F0.5$, but usually $F1$ is used.

Another concept applied in the design of experiments is the so-called baseline. This concept corresponds to a commonly accepted method of the state of the art to solve the same problem and has to be overcome by the proposed hypothesis. Normally, the baseline is not a very sophisticated method. It is also advisable to make a comparison of the proposed method with the more complex methods of the state of the art. Sometimes, baseline methods can be very simple, like, to choose the class randomly or to choose always the majority class.

Since we are talking about the data manually annotated by humans (annotators), which is used for the evaluation of the method, the concept of "gold standard" is introduced. As the data is manually annotated, it is not supposed to contain errors (this is the idea of "gold"), and if the system can reach this standard, it works really well.

An interesting question is related to the agreement between human annotators, i.e., whether humans themselves annotate some linguistic phenomenon differently. If so, we cannot expect a machine to resolve properly this same phenomenon. To measure the agreement among the annotators "kappa statistic" [16] is used.

There is also the concept of the top line, that is, the maximum value that can be obtained by a program, given a mismatch between annotators. In general, it is advisable to ask several annotators to do the job, and not just one, for better reasoned and less biased judgments.

To carry out the experiments the k-fold cross validation technique is commonly used, where k is a numerical value, which normally equals to 10. The technique is to divide all the data sample into 10 (or k) subsamples. First, the subsample 1 is used for the evaluation of the system performance, and the subsamples 2–10 are used for training; then subsample 2 is selected for the evaluation and the other 9 subsamples for training and so on.

Thus, the system is evaluated 10 times on different data and trained 10 times on slightly different data; then the average of the 10 evaluations is taken as the final value. In this way, the effect of fluctuations in the data can be neutralized.

Note that it is very important not to evaluate the performance of the system using the same data on which the system was trained; this is why it is divided into k subsamples. If the same data is used, the learning algorithm can detect the specific characteristics of this data, rather than generalize. This is called overfitting. The overfitting problem is always present in every learning situation, and a number of steps should be taken to prevent it.

To perform all the procedures described, we have to represent the problem formally. Let's briefly overview some of the ideas discussed above. The most commonly used way of representing the objects we are investigating is the vector space model that was discussed in the previous chapters. The problem is represented as a problem of automatic classification in a space, more precisely in a vector space. The objects are represented as sets of features and their values, i.e., each object corresponds to a vector of these values (hence the term "vector space"). This means that each object is a point in the multidimensional space of features. This model is very easy to imagine in the case of two features (two dimensions). For a larger number of dimensions, it is similar.

After constructing the space, a metric is defined in this space. Typically it is the metric of objects similarity defined by the cosine similarity. The idea behind this similarity is the following: the more two objects resemble each other, the more acute the angle between the corresponding vectors in the defined space, and therefore, the greater is the cosine of this angle.

Now, the next question is how to select the features to define the vector space? At this point of our process of designing the experiment, linguistic considerations begin to prevail: it is precisely the linguistic part that determines the features to be selected.

For example, the simplest idea applied in information retrieval is to use all the words in various documents as their features, and then to compare these documents: the more "similar" the words in a pair of documents, the more these documents resemble each other. This is the way of constructing the vector space for the information retrieval task. For measuring "similarity" of words, their *tf–idf* are to be used.

Obviously, in this case, the type of linguistic information that can be used is restricted by the formal requirement of using the vector space model, i.e., it is our obligation to represent objects as sets of features and their values.

The next option commonly used in practice that already has some linguistic justification, is the idea of using n-grams as features in the vector space model. As noted above, the concept of traditional n-gram – words (or other elements) sequences as they appear in a text – has a linguistic justification, that is to introduce the syntagmatic information of words (follow or precede other words).

However, it would have been much more helpful to use an even more "linguistic" knowledge, i.e., that encloses more proper linguistic information. As a path in this direction, in our previous works [93–98], we have proposed a new concept of n-grams, which contains more information of a linguistic nature than traditional n-grams: syntactic n-grams. The idea of syntactic n-grams is to construct those by following paths in syntactic trees. That way, syntactic n-grams remain n-grams, yet allow introducing syntactic information into machine learning methods.

In the next part of the book, we discuss syntactic n-grams as well as some other possibilities of non-linear construction of n-grams: filtered and generalized n-grams.

5.3   Design of Experiments

After considering all the notions mentioned above, we can describe the design of experiments in modern computational linguistics which includes the following steps:

1. Define the task (e.g., automatic summarization, authorship attribution, information retrieval, etc.). Often defining a task which differs from the standard tasks contains an interesting scientific contribution.

2. Select the texts for the design of experiments, which is equivalent to the corpus preparation. Several criteria for texts selection can be used. It is always better to use existing corpora for a given task: it allows more objective interpretation of the results and comparison. However, it is not mandatory: one can always develop the corpus himself. In this case, we recommend making it public so that others could use it as well.

3. Prepare the gold standard. To do this, we have to annotate the corpus (or a part of it) manually. The type of annotation depends on the problem we are solving. It is recommended to base on judgments of several annotators and to calculate the agreement between them to determine the top line.

4. Build the vector space model selecting the features and their values. It is advisable to try several types of features, unigrams, n-grams, syntactic n-grams, as well as various elements they can be composed of (words, lemmas, POS tags, etc.), and several types of values: *tf*, *tf-idf*, etc. Furthermore, we can apply a specific method to make some changes in the standard vector space model. To a large extent, that would be a scientific contribution.

5. Define and implement one or more baseline methods, which are very simple, and one or more methods of the state of the art, which are more complex ones. Of course, all these methods have to tackle the same problem.

6. Select and implement one or more supervised machine learning methods. It is recommended to use the methods already developed, for example, WEKA [45] implements dozens of machine learning methods. At the same time, we have to analyze the parameters of these methods and their ranges in order to subsequently test different combinations of these parameters. As already mentioned, in computational linguistics, the most used methods are Naive Bayes (NB), support vector machines (SVM), and classifier based on decision trees (J48). Nevertheless, we recommend trying as many methods as possible. Moreover, at this point, we have to consider the option of applying the latent semantic analysis (or a similar way of the vector space transformation) to reduce the dimensionality of the problem. LSA is already implemented in WEKA.

7. Convert the textual data into a format accepted by the machine learning methods based on the vector space model built. In the case of WEKA, these are ARFF (attribute relation file format) files.

8. Conduct supervised machine learning experiments: these are the procedures that can be performed by the machine learning methods: they are able to automatically distinguish between several classes defined in the corpus based on the vector space model built. We recommend using the cross validation procedure based on 10 folds (subsamples). Experiments are carried out for the proposed model and compared with the results of the baseline algorithms and with the algorithms of the state of the art.

9. Calculate the values of precision, recall, and especially of $F1$ measure for all of the methods mentioned above and perform a comparison between the methods. If the proposed method gives better results, this method is justified.

At the current stage, the scientific contribution to a considerable extent consists in construction of the vector space model, and some additional procedures that allow the transformation of this model (a specific method proposed by a researcher). To some extent, the scientific contribution may also include the problem definition as well as the analysis that shows which machine learning methods, dimension reduction, and parameters are the best for the selected problem.

This is the current research paradigm. We hope that in the future, more attention will be paid to the development of linguistic features, manual, automatic, or semi-automatic, as it is already being realized in the generative models based on local linguistic features, such as Conditional Random Fields, given that for many tasks they produce better results than the traditional methods.

Chapter 6
Example of Application of n-grams: Authorship Attribution Using Syllables

6.1 Authorship Attribution Task

As we described in the previous chapters, mainstream of the modern computational linguistics is based on application of machine learning methods. We represent our task as a classification task, represent our objects formally using features and their values (constructing vector space model), and then apply well-known classification algorithms. In this pipeline, the crucial question is how to select the features. For example, we can use as features words or n-grams of words (sequences of words) or sequences of characters (character n-grams), etc. An interesting question arises: Can we use syllables as features? It is very rarely done in computational linguistics, but there is certain linguistic reality behind syllables. This chapter explores this possibility for the authorship attribution task; it follows our research paper [99]. Note that syllables are somewhat similar to character n-grams in the sense that they are composed of several characters (being not too long).

The authorship attribution (AA) task aims at determining who authored an anonymous text given text samples of a number of candidate authors [52]. The history of AA research goes back to the late nineteenth century, when [73] studied the disputed authorship among Bacon, Marlowe, and Shakespeare.

In the twentieth century, there were several notorious cases related with the authorship. One of them is *The Federalist* papers published in 1787–1788. They contain 85 essays arguing in favor of the US Constitution, which are considered a remarkable example of political prose. There were three authors of these essays. In 63 cases, the authorship is known, while in other 12 cases, it is disputed, and it was the object of early-stage authorship attribution studies [78].

Another case is if the author of The Gospel of Luke also wrote the Book of Acts. There are opposite points of view. Many arguments are based on theological ideas or circumstantial facts, like was Luke the doctor or not.

G. Sidorov, *Syntactic n-grams in Computational Linguistics*, SpringerBriefs in Computer Science, https://doi.org/10.1007/978-3-030-14771-6_6

Another notable case is the dispute about the authorship of the novel *And Quiet Flows the Don* by Mikhail Sholokhov. Some critics claimed that he was too young at the moment of its writing having just 23 years, while the novel is very mature. It was suggested that the other possible author is Fyodor Kryukov, who also wrote about the life of Cossacks. It was supposed that after the death of F. Kryukov in 1920, M. Sholokhov might have access to his manuscripts and used them. A study in 1977 by Scandinavian scientists using existing at that moment computing tools and techniques (sentence lengths, frequencies of several frequent POS n-grams, etc.) confirms the authorship of M. Sholokhov. Maybe, it is worth trying to compare previous results in these cases with modern authorship attribution approaches based on machine learning.

In recent years, the AA task has experienced an increase in interest due to the growing amount of textual data available on the Internet and a wide range of AA applications: it contributes to marketing, electronic commerce, and security purposes, as well as to terrorism prevention and forensics applications, for example, by limiting the number of candidate authors of a text under investigation [1]. The interest in this task is partly driven by the annual organization of the PAN evaluation campaign[1], which is held as part of the CLEF conference and is considered as the main *fora* for AA and relates tasks on digital text forensics.

There are two common approaches to tackle the AA task: statistical and machine learning. Statistical methods were widely used in earlier studies. They include histograms of word-length distribution of various authors [73], principle component analysis of function words [9], etc. Machine learning approach consists in representing the objects (text samples) as a set of features and their values, that is, building a vector space model (VSM). This model defines a space of N dimensions; each dimension in this space corresponds to a feature. Then a machine learning algorithm is applied to training data to learn to assign class labels (authors' names) to objects (text samples) using previously selected features. Thus, the AA task from a machine learning perspective is targeted as a multi-class, single-label classification problem, in which the set of class labels (authors' names) is defined beforehand.

Authors' writing style is the most important information required for solving AA problems. Character n-grams are considered among the most discriminating stylometric features for both single- and cross-topic AA task [102, 90, 68, 70], as well as for similar tasks, such as author profiling [69], and others. In single-topic AA task, all the authors write about the same topic, while in cross-topic AA the thematic areas of training and test corpora are disjoint [103]. Cross-topic AA is a more realistic scenario to the development of practical applications of this task, since the thematic area of the target anonymous text is often different from the documents available for training a machine learning classifier. One possible explanation of the good performance of character n-gram features is their capacity to capture various aspects of authors' stylistic choices, including lexical and syntactic nuances, as well as punctuation and capitalization information [103, 55].

---

[1] http://pan.webis.de [last access: 27.12.2016]. All other URLs in this document were also verified on this date.

[91] showed that not all categories of character n-grams are equally indicative. They claim that character n-grams that capture information concerning affixes and punctuation marks (morpho-syntactic and stylistic information) are more effective than when using the whole set of character n-grams, that is, when including those n-grams that capture thematic content (word-like n-grams).

One of the challenges when using character n-grams is to determine the optimal size of these features. The size can depend on the language and corpus, as well as on the category of character n-grams [68]. Syllables are able to capture the same information as typed character n-grams, being linguistically adjusted to the appropriate size. It makes it interesting to examine the predictiveness of syllables as features for the task of AA. Moreover, to the best of our knowledge, no work has been done on using syllables as features for this task.

In this chapter, we conduct experiments adopting the categories of character n-grams proposed by [91] to syllables. We examine the predictiveness of these features under single- and cross-topic AA conditions using English corpora, as well as under cross-topic AA conditions using a Spanish dataset. We compare the obtained results with the typed character n-grams approach proposed in [91], with the bag-of-words approach, and with random baseline.

The research questions addressed in this chapter are the following: (1) Can syllables be used as predictive features for single- and cross-topic AA task? and (2) Which categories of syllables are more effective for the English and Spanish languages?

Is the conclusion reported in [91], that for the English language, the best performing model is based solely on affix and punctuation n-grams, valid also for syllables? Is this conclusion valid for the Spanish language?

The remainder of this chapter is organized as follows. First, we describe related work in single- and cross-topic AA. Then we present the procedure of adopting character n-gram categories to syllables. After this, the datasets used in this work are described, and the experimental settings and obtained results are presented. Finally, we draw the conclusions from this work and point to the directions of future work.

6.2   Related Work

Over the last years, a large number of methods have been applied to authorship attribution (AA) problems. Most of the prior work focused on single-topic AA conditions, when texts for training and evaluation are written on the same topic. A great variety of feature types aiming at capturing stylistic properties of author's style, feature representations, and machine learning algorithms were examined for single-topic AA (see [104] for a more detailed overview of single-topic AA studies). Function words [55, 48], part-of-speech n-grams [17], functional lexical features [5], and functions of vocabulary richness [106] are considered to be reliable markers of author's style.

[86] showed that the combination of different feature types improves the performance of the AA models.

[107] introduced a linguistic profiling technique, when counts of linguistic features are considered to compare separate authors to average profiles.

[65] analyzed the effect of using a larger set of authors (145 authors) on feature selection and learning and the effect of using limited training data in the AA task.

[58] introduced the "impostors" method based on repeated feature subsampling methods.

[42] achieved promising results extracting textual patterns based on features obtained from shortest path walks over integrated syntactic graphs. However, a single-topic condition considerably simplifies the realistic scenario of AA problems, since in many realistic situations in which stylometry is applied (e.g., forensics), it is very unlikely to obtain examples of the writing on the same topic and genre.

Recently, the focus of the AA community has shifted toward cross-topic and cross-genre AA conditions [105], which is a more challenging but yet a more realistic scenario to the development of practical applications of this task, since style is affected by both genre and topic. [85] demonstrated that feature representation plays an important role in this task. The authors achieved high performance using doc2vec-based feature representation.

[90] showed that out-of-topic data, that is, training texts from multiple topics instead of a single topic, allows achieving higher results under cross-topic AA conditions.

Various independent studies report a substantial accuracy drop under cross-topic AA conditions when compared to single-topic and single-genre conditions, suggesting that obtaining high cross-topic and cross-genre results remains challenging in AA [105]. Detailed overview of cross-topic and cross-genre AA studies is given in [105].

Several prior studies have demonstrated the predictiveness of character n-gram features both under single- and cross-topic AA conditions [103, 91, 68, 62]. These language-independent stylometric features have proved to provide good results in this task due to their sensitivity to both the content and form of a text, among other reasons [55, 14].

More recently, the work by [91] showed that some categories of character n-grams perform better than others for the English language. The authors concluded that there is no need to consider the whole set of character n-gram features, claiming that excluding word-like n-grams enhances AA accuracy.

6.3   Syllables and Their Use in Authorship Attribution

Most of the studies in AA [24, 43] and other natural language processing (NLP) tasks, author profiling [83], text cohesion and text difficulty estimation [71], and automatic readability assessment [21], among others, that explore syllables, use the average number of syllables per word as features and not syllables as such.

Reviewing the AA-related literature, we did not encounter any mentions of using syllables as features for this task nor for related tasks. This makes it important to study the impact of syllables and different categories of syllables in single- and cross-topic AA. The assessment of their performance in the English and Spanish languages is the basis of the main research question addressed in this work.

The absence of application of syllables in the tasks of the computational linguistics is surprising especially if we compare it with the wide use of character n-grams. In fact, syllables are a linguistic reality; especially it is a psycholinguistic reality. Say, when a person starts learning to read, he usually is composing letters into syllables. On the other hand, the first phonetic writing systems were based on syllables, which later turned into letters corresponding to single sounds.

We will not discuss in this chapter the definition of syllables. Note that we are dealing with the written texts, so for our purposes it is sufficient to have some syllabification rules. Further we consider various types of syllables depending on the word structure (position of a syllable in a word), similar to typed/untyped character n-grams.

6.4 Untyped and Typed Syllables

In this work, the same categories of character n-grams as introduced in [91] are applied to syllables. All character n-grams and syllables are grouped into three super categories (affix-, word-, and punctuation-related n-grams/syllables). The definitions of the categories of character n-grams and syllables are provided below. We slightly refine some of the original definitions of character n-gram categories provided in [91], with the aim of making them more accurate. Thus, the categories of character n-grams are the following:

Affix character n-grams

prefix: An n-gram that covers the first n characters of a word that is at least n + 1 characters long.

suffix: An n-gram that covers the last n characters of a word that is at least n + 1 characters long.

space-prefix: An n-gram that begins with a space and that does not contain any punctuation mark.

space-suffix: An n-gram that ends with a space, that does not contain any punctuation mark, and whose first character is not a space.

Word character n-grams

whole-word: An n-gram that encompasses all the characters of a word and that is exactly n characters long.

mid-word: An n-gram that contains n characters of a word that is at least n + 2 characters long and that does not include neither the first nor the last character of the word.

multi-word: An n-gram that spans multiple words, identified by the presence of a space in the middle of the n-gram.

Punctuation character n-grams (abbreviated as punct)

beg-punct: An n-gram whose first character is a punctuation mark, but the middle characters are not.

mid-punct: An n-gram whose middle character is a punctuation mark.

end-punct: An n-gram whose last character is punctuation, but the first and the middle characters are not.

The similar categories of syllables are the following:

Affix syllables

prefix: First syllable of a word that has at least two syllables.

suffix: Last syllable of a word that has at least two syllables[2].

Word syllables

whole-word: One-syllable word.

mid-word: Middle syllables of a word that have at least three syllables.

multi-word: Last syllable of a word and first syllable of the next word.

Punctuation syllables (abbreviated as punct)

beg-punct: A punctuation mark followed by first syllable of the next word.

mid-punct: Last syllable of a word followed by a punctuation mark followed by first syllable of the next word.

end-punct: Last syllable of a word followed by a punctuation mark.

Tables 6.1 and 6.2 show the extracted character n-grams and syllables, respectively, when applying the proposed categories to the following sample sentence:

(1) *She said, "My mother will arrive tomorrow night."*

We examine three models of syllables, using the models applied by Sapkota et al. [91] to character n-grams. Note that we use different feature sets (syllables) in each case, i.e., we obtained these feature sets in different manner.

All-untyped: when the categories of syllables are ignored; any distinct syllable is a different feature.

All-typed: when syllables of all available categories (*affix* + *word* + *punct*) are considered.

Affix + Punct: when the syllables of the *word* category are excluded.

The conclusion of [91] was that in the English language, models based on *affix + punct* features were more efficient than models trained using all the features. In this chapter, these three models were applied in order to examine whether this conclusion is also valid for syllables; moreover, we examine whether this conclusion is also valid for the Spanish language.

---

[2] For syllables, space-prefix and space-suffix categories are omitted since they correspond to prefix and suffix categories.

Table 6.1 Character n-grams (n = 3) per category for the sample sentence (1), where SC stands for Super Category

SC	Category	Character trigrams
Affix	*prefix*	*sai mot wil arr tom nig*
	suffix	*aid her ill ive row ght*
	space-prefix	*_sa _mo _wi _ar _to _ni*
	space-suffix	*he_ My_ er_ ll_ ve_ ow_*
Word	*whole-word*	*She*
	mid-word	*oth the rri riv omo mor orr rro igh*
	multi-word	*e_s y_m r_w l_a e_t w_n*
Punct	*beg-punct*	*,_" "My*
	mid-punct	*d,_ "M_ t."*
	end-punct	*id, ht*

Table 6.2 Syllables per category for the sample sentence (1), where SC stands for Super Category

SC	Category	Syllables
Affix	*prefix*	*moth ar to*
	suffix	*er rive row*
Word	*whole-word*	*She said My will night*
	mid-word	*mor*
	multi-word	*She_said My_moth er_will will_ar rive_to row_night*
Punct	*beg-punct*	*"My*
	mid-punct	*–*
	end-punct	*said, night*

6.5 Datasets

We conduct two sets of experiments using (i) English single- and cross-topic corpora and (ii) using Spanish cross-topic corpus. In case of English, we use the same datasets as in [91]. That is, for single-topic experiments, we use a subset of the Reuters Corpus Volume 1 [62], which consists of corporate news written by 10 different authors with 100 newswire stories per author on the same thematic area. Following [91], balanced training and test settings of this corpus were considered. We refer to this single-topic English corpus as CCAT 10. For cross-topic experiments in English, we used *The Guardian* corpus. This corpus is composed of opinion articles published in *The Guardian* newspaper in four thematic areas (Politics, Society, World, and the UK). The texts were written by 13 different authors. Following previous studies [103, 91], ten documents per author were considered for each of the four thematic areas.

A new cross-topic Spanish corpus was built automatically using crawler developed in the Python programming language. Given a set of URL seeds, the crawler extracted the names of the authors and the corresponding articles from the news website Cultura Colectiva[3]. The developed Spanish corpus consists of articles written

---

[3] http://CulturaCollectiva.com

Table 6.3 Number of documents written by authors on six topics for the Spanish corpus

Author #	Cinema	Food	Photo.	Art	Design	Lifestyle	Total per author
Author 1	52	16	16	22	9	34	149
Author 2	51	16	17	31	12	54	181
Author 3	26	5	21	18	44	33	147
Author 4	6	4	9	13	5	14	51
Author 5	14	7	4	13	8	12	58
Author 6	9	2	7	12	12	15	57
Total per topic	158	50	74	109	90	162	–

Table 6.4 Statistics of the CCAT 10, *The Guardian*, and Spanish corpus

Corpus	#authors	#docs/author/topic	#sentences/doc	#words/doc
CCAT 10	10	100	19	425
The Guardian	13	13	53	1034
Spanish corpus	6	See Table 6.3	36	962

in six thematic areas (Cinema, Food, Photography, Art, Design, and Lifestyle) by six different authors. We did not construct similar corpus for single-topic condition for Spanish, since we did not have enough resources for this. We preferred cross-topic condition, which is the modern trend.

The corpus is unbalanced in terms of documents written by authors on six topics (Table 6.3), since the use of a balanced subset of the corpus was not feasible due to a very short number of authors with a relevant number of texts in all six considered topics. Therefore, the developed cross-topic Spanish corpus addresses more challenging but at the same time more realistic AA conditions, when the same number of text samples written by different authors is not available.

Table 6.4 shows some of the statistics of the CCAT 10, *The Guardian*, and Spanish corpus.

To perform tokenization, we used Natural Language Toolkit[4] tokenizer.

6.6   Automatic Syllabification

After analyzing existing modules for syllabic division for both English and Spanish (Pyphen[5], PyHyphen[6], and Hyphenate[7]), we noticed that a large number of words encountered in the corpora are not present in the dictionaries of these modules and/or are divided incorrectly into syllables. Therefore, we decided to use existing

---

[4] http://www.nltk.org

[5] https://pypi.python.org/pypi/Pyphen

[6] https://pypi.python.org/pypi/PyHyphen

[7] https://pypi.python.org/pypi/hyphenate

Table 6.5 Statistics about the dictionaries used for syllabic division

Corpus	N of words in corpus	N of words encountered in the dictionary	% of words encountered in the dictionary
CCAT 10	20,073	13,747	68.49%
The Guardian	25,518	21,680	84.96%
Spanish corpus	36,995	23,049	62.30%

lexical resources in order to perform syllabic division. Thus, for the English language, we used Moby Hyphenator[8], which contains 186,097 hyphenated entries. If a word encountered in the corpus is not present in the Moby Hyphenator, we used alternative lexical resources that allow syllabic division[9]. For the Spanish language, we used the dictionary of syllabic division OSLIN-Es[10], which contains 110,527 hyphenated entries. Table 6.5 presents some statistics on how many words (%) were encountered in the dictionaries for each of the three considered corpora.

It is clear that the syllabification techniques with dictionaries do not cover the whole set of words (see Table 6.5). Thus, we applied a heuristic for extension of the coverage based on the morphological structure of the words. We considered the sets of prefixes and suffixes for English and Spanish languages and used them for division into syllables. This method of division is justified by the idea that we are interested in typed syllables related to affixes. This heuristic allowed to improve the coverage up to 90%.

Another consideration with respect to the coverage is that the words that are not in the mentioned dictionaries should be relatively rare words or named entities. So we expect that their influence on authorship attribution is minimal.

Probably, simpler heuristic based on phonetical rules would give better results, for example, division into syllables using just positions of vowels or combinations of vowels. We leave this option for future work.

6.7 Experimental Methodology

In this chapter, we apply standard methodology based on application of machine learning methods, as described in Chap. 5: (1) we represent our task as classification problem; (2) then we select the features and their values (i.e., we construct vector space model (VSM)); (3) further we prepare the data (corpus), which is marked with necessary information (in our case, it is just the author of each text); and (4) finally, we apply traditional machine learning algorithms (like Naive Bayes or support

---

[8] http://icon.shef.ac.uk/Moby/mhyph.html

[9] https://www.howmanysyllables.com; https://ahdictionary.com; http://www.dictionary.com

[10] http://es.oslin.org/syllables.php

vector machines, which allow for evaluation of results: typically, calculation of accuracy or F1-measure) over the marked corpus using features from the VSM.

One of the evaluation schemes, which we applied in this chapter, consists in dividing the data into training and test sets. Then the machine learning algorithm learns from the training set and makes decisions for further evaluation over the test set. Note that these two sets should always be different, otherwise overfitting occurs. Other possible approach to evaluation is k-fold cross-validation.

Another important part of research is comparison with other methods from state-of-the-art or baseline methods. As the baseline, usually a very simple ("silly") method is applied, for example, random selection or selection of the majoritarian class.

One of the most traditional approaches using machine learning in text-related tasks is to use words as features in the VSM. This is called bag-of-words model (BoW). It is "bag" in the sense that there are no relations between words; they all are independent. This supposition of independency, which is too strong, is usually overcome in other models, for example, by using n-grams of various types. Note that bag-of-words approach is commonly considered as a strong method for AA and related tasks [50, 67, 68], though it is relatively simple and computationally inexpensive method.

Now let us describe the application of this general scheme to our task.

AA as a classification problem As we already mentioned, authorship attribution task from a machine learning perspective is targeted as a multi-class, single-label classification problem, in which the set of class labels (authors' names) is defined beforehand. Our objects are texts; their labels are the authors. Note that there can be many authors, i.e., it is multi-class problem. We learn from the texts with the known authorship (training data), and then we should decide the author of the new texts (test data).

Feature selection This is central point of the machine learning approaches. [91] used for the same task case-sensitive typed character n-grams of length 3 and considered only those features that occur at least five times in the training corpus. Note that this is the full description of the model that they used. We used the same approach with the same threshold for the frequency, but instead of typed character n-grams, we use various types of character n-grams obtained from syllables as described in Sect. 6.3.

Data preparation We use three corpora marked with authors of the texts, one for single-topic and two for cross-topic authorship attribution, as described in Sect. 6.4.

Application of machine learning algorithms As in [91], we used WEKA's [45] implementation of support vector machines (SVM) for classification. SVM classifier has been shown to be effective for the AA task and was the classifier of choice under cross-topic conditions at PAN 2015 [105].

Evaluation of experiments Each model is evaluated in terms of accuracy on the test corpus. For publicly available single-topic corpus CCAT 10, the division into test and training data is already established. So, we just performed the evaluation over the existing data. For cross-topic experiments, testing is performed on one topic, while training on the rest of topics. This procedure is repeated for each topic, and the results are averaged. We carried out experiments applying three models described in Sect. 6.3 to syllables. These models correspond to the categories of features: *all-untyped*, *all-typed*, and *affix + punctuation*.

Comparison We used the variation of the bag-of-words approach, when punctuation marks are excluded, that is, we considered only the frequency of the words. Next, we conducted experiments using character 3-grams. We applied the algorithm of [91] to the three corpora described above. Though we implemented the algorithm following as exactly as possible the description, the obtained results on the CCAT 10 and *The Guardian* corpora are slightly different (less than 1%). Correspondingly, we compare the results obtained using syllables with our own implementation of the algorithm of [91]. We also compare with random baselines (see next section).

6.8 Experimental Results

The results in terms of classification accuracy using the bag-of-words baseline, three models of character 3-grams and syllables on the CCAT 10, *The Guardian*, and the Spanish corpus are shown in Table 6.6[11]. Note that all the results are much superior as compared to random baseline (and they are good in this sense, i.e., all methods have reasonable performance). Say, if we have ten authors (CCAT 10 corpus), the random baseline, i.e., assigning the author by chance, is 10%. In *The Guardian* corpus, we have 13 authors, so the random baseline is 7.7%. In Spanish corpus, there are six authors, so the baseline is 16.7%. In Table 6.6, we show the results using bag-of-words approach and three models (*untyped*, *typed*, and *affix + punctuation*) of character n-grams and syllables. The best accuracy for each dataset is highlighted in bold typeface and underlined; the result of the second best method is highlighted.

In Table 6.7 we present the number of features used in each experiment. Number of features is the number of dimensions in the corresponding vector space model: for bag-of-words, it is the number of words used as features; for character n-grams or syllables, it is the number of n-grams or syllables of the corresponding type. It is important that though these numbers are large (from 2000 to 17,000), they are still tractable, i.e., they are not too large, like hundreds of thousands of features, which would be intractable. Let us remind that for character n-grams, we used the threshold

---

[11] Programming of the method was performed by H. J. Hernández and E. López.

Table 6.6 Accuracy (%) of the results on the CCAT 10, *The Guardian*, and Spanish corpus

Approach	All-untyped	All-typed	Affix + punct
CCAT 10			
Random baseline	10.0	–	–
Bag-of-words	76.2	–	–
Char. n-grams	78.2	78.0	**78.8**
Syllables (our)	**76.6**	77.0	72.8
The Guardian			
Random baseline	7.7	–	–
Bag-of-words	46.0	–	–
Char. n-grams	**52.5**	50.0	52.3
Syllables (our)	50.1	45.0	**58.1**
Spanish corpus			
Random baseline	16.7	–	–
Bag-of-words	**55.1**	–	–
Char. n-grams	56.0	56.3	**56.5**
Syllables (our)	54.2	54.8	52.9

Table 6.7 Number of features used in the CCAT 10, *The Guardian*, and Spanish corpus

Approach	All-untyped	All-typed	Affix + punct
CCAT 10			
Bag-of-words	5,166	–	–
Char. n-grams	9,258	10,859	6,296
Syllables (our)	16,991	18,826	5,497
The Guardian			
Bag-of-words	2,595	–	–
Char. n-grams	5,728	6,903	3,779
Syllables (our)	7,947	2,691	2,201
Spanish corpus			
Bag-of-words	2,087	–	–
Char. n-grams	4,914	5,735	3,005
Syllables (our)	5,802	6,420	1,821

for frequency (more than five appearances). Note that the information of the number of features is useful for comparison of machine learning methods, but it is mainly supplementary information. It is worth noting that the size of the feature set is larger when using syllables, except for the case of *affix + punctuation*, when the size is 15–30% less.

It is well-known that the results in cross-topic scenario are lower than in single-topic conditions, because it is much more difficult to make authorship attribution using cross-topic data. For example, in modern competitions on authorship attribution (like PAN), only cross-topic scenario is considered as being more challenging. The reason of this major difficulty is the radical changes in the vocabulary: for a new topic, the authors do not use the majority of words corresponding to a previous topic. This tendency is also observed in our results: there is about 20% of difference in the results for CCAT 10 (single-topic) and for the other two corpora (cross-topic).

For the English language, our approach outperforms the bag-of-words method. On one corpus (CCAT 10), we obtained lower results than those obtained with character 3-grams (difference 2.2%), while on the other one, *The Guardian*, we won by 5.8%. This result is obtained using *affix + punctuation* features. The other feature types are slightly worse for syllables.

For Spanish, the results obtained using syllables are lower than both the BoW method and the character 3-grams approach, but the difference is very small (0.3% for BoW and 1.8% for character n-grams).

Speaking about character 3-grams, *affix + punctuation* is the best model for this type of features on two of the three corpora, but the difference is less than 1%. Thus, the supposition of [91] is valid for the Spanish language, but it is not conclusive since the difference is rather small. Thus, we cannot confirm that it will always hold.

It is worth noting that our syllabification techniques do not cover the whole set of words (see Table 6.5), and though we further applied heuristic based on the morphological structure, which augmented the coverage to 90% of words, better syllabification methods should be applied in future.

Chapter 7
Deep Learning and Vector Space Model

In recent years, a novel paradigm appeared related to application of neural networks to any tasks related to artificial intelligence [59], in particular, in natural language processing [39]. It became extremely popular in NLP area after works of Mikolov et al. starting in 2013 [74, 75]. The main idea of this paradigm is to apply neural networks for automatic learning of relevant features with various levels of generalization in vector space model. Sometimes this model of representation of objects is called continuous vector space model. In general, this paradigm is called "deep learning." It is "deep" in the sense that neural networks learn some deep dependences and relations, which are not present at the surface level. Also, hidden layers of neural networks are used, which also contributes to the term "deep."

In general, neural networks are classifiers (i.e., they solve classification tasks), which are inspired in processing performed by human brain. They are non-linear classifiers, and their most prominent feature is that they are good in generalizations. One of the reasons why this idea only recently came to the real world is because neural networks finally began to function in more or less acceptable time due to the development of the corresponding hardware (GPU arrays).

Speaking more technically, neural network is about activation of neurons according to the input and the weights between them. A network contains input layer, output layer, and several hidden layers. Neurons at each layer are connected to the neurons at the next and the previous layers. These connections have weights (numerical values). The number of neurons at each layer can be different; usually, the closer we are to the output, the smaller is the number of neurons, which corresponds to generalization. The activation is propagated from the input layer to the output layer through the hidden layers. The neurons have activation threshold and are either activated or not. The decision (choice of the class) is made according to the neuron of the output layer with the highest weight. Note that in a real-world deep learning system, we are speaking about hundreds of millions of weights and similar number of learning samples [59].

© The Author(s), under exclusive license to Springer Nature Switzerland AG 2019
G. Sidorov, *Syntactic n-grams in Computational Linguistics*, SpringerBriefs
in Computer Science, https://doi.org/10.1007/978-3-030-14771-6_7

The network works in many cycles (makes many repetitions). First, it propagates the activation forward (starting from the input layer, i.e., input data) and makes the decision. Then it propagates the error in this decision backward (backpropagation) and corrects the weights of the neuron connections [60]. That is, there are many repetitions of classification process, and after each classification is finished, the error in classification is propagated back, and the weights of the connections between neurons are corrected correspondingly. In this way, neural network automatically learns the best weights for the solution.

The input layer encodes the data that we have. According to the input data, the neurons at each layer are activated or not taking into account the weights of their connections (activation is propagated forward). The output layer has the number of neurons that corresponds to the number of classes in our task, i.e., after classification process, a neuron with the maximum activation value represents the result of the classification.

It is necessary to mention that the neurons of the each level of the network represent different levels of generalization. For example, if we consider the task of image recognition, then neurons at some level can represent lines; neurons at the next level can represent forms like rectangular, square, etc., and neurons at the next level are used for more complex objects like houses, faces, or trees, i.e., combinations of more simple forms.

In deep learning, one of the main problems is overfitting. Overfitting is over adjustment of a system to the data. When it happens, the system works perfectly at the data, but does not generalize and will not work well on the new data. There are many techniques that aim to prevent overfitting. In neural networks, we basically try to make the network to forget some details and preserve the correct answer, i.e., to fit into more general situations; see, for example, Hinton et al. [47].

One of the most famous resources related to deep learning in natural language processing is Word2Vec, which contains vectors of 300 dimensions for each word as developed by Mikolov et al. [74, 75]. The principal idea of Word2Vec is to consider the neurons of the penultimate level (which is before the output level, i.e., the ultimate hidden level), i.e., the neurons that will make a decision, as features in the vector space model. In this sense, we need to train a network for each object that we have.

These vectors were trained on very large corpus (Google textual data) using the ideas of the distributional semantics, which uses the words in the context as features for training (i.e., features in the vector space model are the context words taken from the specific window near the given word). It is modern interpretation of the famous idea of J. R. Firth "You shall know a word by the company it keeps" [23].

We would like to stress that deep learning approach in its essence keeps being vector space model. We always obtain the input data in its vector form and apply classification techniques to it. But it is especially clear when we use the idea of using the ultimate hidden level as vector of feature values (continuous vector space model). In this case, the most common operation in this model is calculation of similarity of objects using, for example, cosine similarity. We can also keep applying all machine learning algorithms as we did before.

There are two principal differences with traditional vector space model representations. The first difference is that in traditional vector space model, we have extremely sparse representation, i.e., each object has several nonzero values, meanwhile the rest of the values are zero (say, hundreds nonzeros vs thousands zeros). On the contrary, for neural networks, the values are always real numbers (usually in the interval [0,1]), so they practically never become zeros. Thus, each object has some value for any feature. In this sense, we can compare deep learning with latent semantic analysis: there are not so many dimensions, and these dimensions have nonzero values.

The second difference is related to selection of features. Till now, we considered the representation of objects using their features and values of these features, which were selected by researchers. With deep learning, we decide the architecture of the neural network, and the network chooses automatically the weights of the neurons, which is equivalent to the values of the features. Since the neurons represent different levels of generalization, the network works really well.

The problem with deep learning is that we cannot interpret in natural way what real-world features correspond to neurons. This is the common problem of neural networks: there is no natural interpretation of their results; thus, a system cannot give an explanation of its decisions.

Deep learning is currently widely used with very promising results. In many real-world problems, it outperforms traditional machine learning approaches (though not in every problem). In our opinion, the task of computational linguists related to deep learning is to consider various representations of the input data, for example, n-grams of various types and syntactic n-grams as well.

Part II
Non-linear Construction of n-grams

Chapter 8
Syntactic n-grams: The Concept

8.1 The Idea of Syntactic n-grams

As we have already mentioned, the main idea of the formal features applicable in computational linguistics is related to the vector space model and the use of n-grams as features in this space, which also includes unigrams, i.e., words.

Recall that traditional n-grams are sequences of textual elements (words, lemmas, POS tags, etc.) in the order of their appearance in a text. Traditional n-grams represent syntagmatic information, and they are widely and successfully used in various computational linguistics tasks. Traditional n-grams ignore syntactic knowledge, and they are based solely on syntagmatic information; the established relation is "follow another word." The next question is how can we keep on using the n-grams technique, which is known to give good results and, at the same time, introduce syntactic information? The solution proposed in this book is the special manner of obtaining n-grams – non-linear manner. Our general proposal is to construct n-grams following paths in syntax trees.

Intuitively, we still deal with n-grams but avoid the noise introduced by the surface structure of the language. This type of noise may occur, because syntactically unrelated words may appear together on the surface level. We can tackle this phenomenon if we follow the actual syntactic relations that link the words, even though those words are not immediate neighbors.

Note that in this chapter, we propose to obtain a syntactic n-gram as a fragment of a continuous path; we do not consider bifurcations (returns, interruptions) in the path: the examples are provided below. In the following chapters, we present the concept of non-continuous syntactic n-grams (the general concept), where following the path in a syntax tree allows entering the bifurcations and going back.

So, for now we continue with the description of syntactic n-grams we call "continuous" in order to illustrate the concept of a syntactic n-gram as such. n-grams are "continuous" in the sense that from any node on the path, it is possible to move to a next node in a unique manner.

G. Sidorov, *Syntactic n-grams in Computational Linguistics*, SpringerBriefs in Computer Science, https://doi.org/10.1007/978-3-030-14771-6_8

One can see that it is precisely a non-linear manner of n-grams construction, as the elements are not taken in accordance with their linear order. In this case, the idea of linear order refers to the surface level of a text, where the elements necessarily have to follow each other: recall F. de Saussure's linear nature of the signifier.

Often the term "syntactic n-gram" implies that an n-gram is composed of POS tags, for example, in [1]. We believe that it is a misuse of the term, since POS tags represent not syntactic but morphological information. Syntactic information is used for the POS disambiguation; however, it does not justify the use of the term in this way.

An idea somewhat similar to ours has been proposed by [13]: to use the concept of *skip*-grams (jump-grams), i.e., to randomly form sequences of elements skipping some of them. It is clearly a non-linear construction; however, the n-grams constructed this way contain more noise than the traditional n-grams, and furthermore, their number becomes too large.

A modification of this idea is to use not all *skip*-grams but only those with higher frequencies [46], called "maximal frequent sequences." However, very sophisticated algorithms are required for constructing these sequences (and the problem is np-complete), and there is still a problem of their interpretation: the linguistic reality that corresponds to them does not go beyond finding certain combinations of words.

The other ideas presented in this book on how to build n-grams in a non-linear manner are related to the concepts of filtered n-grams – e.g., using the *tf-idf* of n-grams as a filter *before* the construction of n-grams and generalized n-grams. Say, for the generalized n-grams, we can always use the first word in the list of synonyms (synset) or to promote the words in an ontology to more general concepts, and then we can replace the words for these concepts and construct the n-grams out of these more general concepts.

It is noteworthy that the idea of using structural information concerning relations between words in specific tasks has been already presented in [6, 44, 56]; however, none of these works has been widespread nor associated with the idea of n-grams.

The work [82] proposes a similar idea in the field of semantic analysis, where the utility of syntactic information is shown for very specific tasks of:

1. Semantic priming, i.e., psycholinguistic experiments on words similarity
2. Synonymy detection in TOEFL tests
3. Ordering word senses according to their importance

In our opinion, this work does not have much response in other NLP tasks, precisely because the authors do not relate syntactic information to n-grams, which is the main tool in the vast majority of tasks, nor show its utility in other tasks that are not so specifically semantics oriented.

For the illustration of the concept of syntactic n-grams let us consider, as an example, two sentences taken from a book by Jules Verne. The first example is in the Spanish language, and the second one is in the English language. For the both examples, the syntactic tree is built in advance, i.e., we have syntactic information represented in terms of dependency grammars.

8.2 Previous Ideas Related to Application of Syntactic Information

Now let us discuss the history of appearance and development of the idea of the syntactic n-grams. Obviously, the idea to use syntactic relations as an additional information in solution of a certain problem is not new. Below we mention several works, which used this idea. Nevertheless, all of them were centered on the specific solution and usually consider a specific type of n-gram, restricted by size (two or three elements) or by type (use only POS tags, or use only words and the syntactic relations between them). We can call these works the predecessors of the idea of syntactic n-grams. No generalizations were presented, nor specific general-purpose metalanguage was proposed, same as typology of syntactic n-grams was not considered. Also, it should be mentioned that none of these works considered the general task of machine learning and the possibility to use syntactic n-grams as features directly, similar to traditional n-grams. Probably this is the reason why the term "syntactic n-grams" was never used in these works.

There is also another work by Y. Goldberg and J. Orwant (2013) [40], which was developed when the leading author was at the research stay at Google. This work appeared practically at the same time with the papers by the author of the book on the subject, but a little bit later. The term syntactic n-gram was also used in this work (at that moment the term by [40] was "syntactic-Ngram," which was changed later). Obviously, this work was completely independent from ours, but interestingly it appeared practically at the same time: the scientific ideas flow in the air. We will describe this work further in this section.

It is interesting to mention that the predecessor works are basically divided into four categories:

– Works for learning word properties based on their contexts (distributional semantics)
– Works for information extraction
– Works for learning selectional preferences
– Works for improvement of dependency parsing

It is quite clear that learning selectional preferences or improvement of dependency parsing are directly related with syntactic information. So, it is very natural that these tasks rely on syntactic paths.

In very similar manner in information extraction, the data is often represented as tuples, like *<subject, verb, object>*. In order to obtain this data, it is also very natural to use dependency information between words, because it helps a lot in obtaining these tuples [3]. The author of this book was the director of a thesis using this idea since 2011, and the corresponding paper was published [3].

In distributional semantics, on the other hand, our goal is to describe a word using the context words. We usually construct a matrix for words considering as features the words that appear in their near context. Well, in this sense, syntactic information can help in choosing the words that conform "real" context, i.e., that have direct syntactic relations with the word itself or its dependent words.

Once again, we would like to stress that none of these approaches made the generalization for general situation of machine learning, and all of them have specific reasons for considering syntactic information, as it constitutes an important part of the problem itself, unlike the general situation of features selection, when we can use either traditional n-grams or syntactic n-grams.

It should be mentioned that the idea of bypassing syntactic trees for obtaining information for pragmatic level of the language (dialog, logical structure) was used in works [26–29].

Works on distributional semantics
Probably the first work related to exploitation of the syntactic information in specific tasks is by Lin (1998) [63]. The author considers the task of calculation of word similarity based on the context. As the context, he uses triplets of words, which also include names of syntactic relations between them as well.

The other work by Lin and Pantel (2001) [64] is about discovery of inference rules from text, for example, inference relations (X wrote Y = X is author of Y). Distributional hypothesis is applied to paths in dependency trees, not words.

One more work aimed at distributional semantics is by Padó and Lapata (2007) [82]. The main idea is to use dependency-based features in construction of semantic space models. They suppose that syntactic structures reflect lexical meaning (verb arguments). They include as features the path, its length, and also adds weights. The main purpose of the paper is selection of the correct context.

A work similar to the previous one by Baroni and Lenci (2010) [8] presents a distributional memory, where syntactic relations form part of the distributional representation. In this case, very much similar to information extraction, phrases are converted into tuples, "a set of weighted word-link-word tuples arranged into a third-order tensor," for example, "*The soldier became sergeant → <sergeant, predicate noun, become>.*"

Works on selectional preferences
We will mention just some of the works on selectional preferences, for example, [19, 20]. In these works, the authors present "structured vector space model that addresses these issues by incorporating the selectional preferences for words' argument positions." In this manner, they integrate syntax into the computation of word meaning in context. Thus, this vector space model contains vectors representing the word's selectional preferences.

Works on information extraction
One of the representative works on information extraction is the work by Wu and Weld, when Wikipedia is used for open information extraction (2010) [108]. They use generalized paths of tuples including names of syntactic relations, for example, *N-nsubj-V-dobj-N*. There are several IE works that are based on syntactic parsing, even syntactic kernels are proposed for this purpose. In our opinion, it is better to treat syntax on the level of features and not on the level of kernels.

Works on improvement of dependency parsing

The work by Chen et al. (2009) [12] proposes improving dependency parsing with sub-trees from auto-parsed data. They construct new subtree-based features for parsing algorithms. Only sub-trees for bigrams (first order) and trigrams (second order) are considered. Another manner of improving dependency parsing is presented in Sagae and Gordon (2009) [89], where syntactic similarity of words based on paths in parse tree is considered. It helps parsing of the predicate-argument structures.

Google book of syntactic n-grams

As we mentioned before in this section, the work by Goldberg and Orwant (2013) [40] also presents the idea of syntactic n-grams and introduce the term (as "syntactic-Ngrams"). They develop a very large set of syntactic n-grams for very many books in English through time (for different time periods). This work was developed at Google and published in 2013. Our first publication related to syntactic n-grams appeared on the Web in September 2012. Still, it is quite clear that this work is independent from ours. It should be also mentioned that the primary idea of that work was to consider the changes in the word combinations (obtained using syntactic information). The authors did not consider the general situation of machine learning. Also, the fact that we do have the historical information of n-grams for many books will not help us to solve our specific problem if we plan to apply feature selection and machine learning. On the contrary, our goal was to apply it in specific tasks as features, and our source code for extraction of syntactic n-grams was available for all users from the very beginning, so it was possible to apply it in any task.

It is also interesting to mention that when the author of the book talked about the term "syntactic n-grams" to someone, the first reaction was "you mean n-grams of POS tags," as, for example, in [2]. This is not correct in a strict sense, because POS tags represent morphosyntactic information. For now, the term "syntactic n-grams" is much more accepted, for example, we have more than 450 citations at our works starting from 2012.

8.3 Example of Continuous Syntactic n-grams in Spanish

The parser of the FreeLing system [10, 80, 81] is used to parse the Spanish example. The syntactic dependencies are shown through the indented analysis result, i.e., the blocks with the same indentation have the same main word (if another possible main word does not appear among those words). The sentence in Spanish is the following:

El doctor Ferguson se ocupaba desde hacía mucho tiempo de todos los pormenores de su expedición. (lit: *The Dr. Ferguson has been engaged upon all the details of his expedition since a long time ago.*) *"Dr. Ferguson had long been engaged upon the details of his expedition."*

The FreeLing parser generates the following output in terms of dependency grammars:

```
grup-verb/top/(ocupaba ocupar VMII1S0 -) [
  morfema-verbal/es/(se se P0000000 -)
  sn/subj/(doctor doctor NCMS000 -) [
    espec-ms/espec/(El el DA0MS0 -)
    w-ms/sn-mod/(Ferguson ferguson NP00000 -)
  ]
  prep/modnomatch/(desde desde SPS00 -)
  grup-verb/modnomatch/(hacía hacer VMII1S0 -) [
    sn/cc/(tiempo tiempo NCMS000 -) [
      espec-ms/espec/(mucho mucho DI0MS0 -)
      sp-de/sp-mod/(de de SPS00 - ) [
        sn/obj-prep/(pormenores pormenor NCMP000 -) [
          espec-mp/espec/(todos todo DI0MP0 -) [
            j-mp/espec/(los el DA0MP0 -)
          ]
        ]
      ]
      sp-de/sp-mod/(de de SPS00 - ) [
        sn/obj-prep/(expedición expedición NCFS000 -) [
          espec-fs/espec/(su su DP3CS0 -)
        ]
      ]
    ]
    F-term/term/(..Fp -)
  ]
]
```

The corresponding tree is illustrated in Figs. 8.1 and 8.2. It can be seen that the parser committed several errors. For example, it placed the groups of words *de su expedición* "*of his expedition*" and *de todos los pormenores* "upon all the details" as dependents of the word *tiempo* "time" instead of the verb *ocuparse* "*engage.*" Parsers can commit such errors due to various types of syntactic ambiguity, which is difficult to solve automatically. Nevertheless, in many cases, this does not significantly affect the system performance, since the vast majority of dependencies are established correctly, and these errors are not severe enough to ruin the tree structure. In the tree below, we indicate the parser errors with dotted lines. Moreover, for the automatic processing, the output format of this parser is not very handy.

We have developed a software that converts the FreeLing output format into another format, which is similar to the one of the Stanford parser. The software is freely available on the author's personal web page.

We present the result of the format conversion below. Note that in this case, the word numbers correspond to the lines in the output generated by the FreeLing parser and not to the actual numbers of their positions in the sentence.

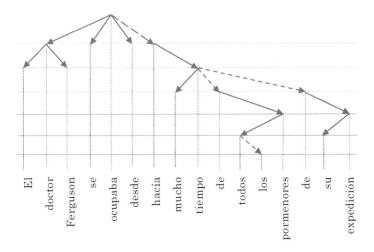

Fig. 8.1 Example of a syntax tree in Spanish

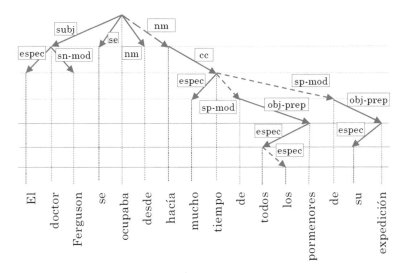

Fig. 8.2 Example of a syntax tree with tags in Spanish

```
top(root-0, ocupaba-1)
es(ocupaba-1, se-2)
subj(ocupaba-1, doctor-3)
espec(doctor-3, el-4)
sn-mod(doctor-3, Ferguson-5)
modnomatch(ocupaba-1, desde-6)
modnomatch(ocupaba-1, hacía-7)
cc(hacía-7, tiempo-8)
```

```
espec(tiempo-8, mucho-9)
sp-mod(tiempo-8, de-10)
obj-prep(de-10, pormenores-11)
espec(pormenores-11, todos-12)
espec(todos-12, los-13)
sp-mod(tiempo-8, de-14)
obj-prep(de-14, expedición-15)
espec(expedición-15, su-16)
```

Using the tree, we can obtain the following continuous syntactic n-grams.
The bigrams are the following:

ocupaba se "*engaged*"
ocupaba doctor "*engaged dr.*"
doctor el "dr. the"
doctor ferguson "dr. ferguson"
ocupaba desde "engaged since"
ocupaba hacía "engaged ago"
hacía tiempo "ago time"
tiempo mucho "time long"
tiempo de "time upon"
de pormenores "upon details"
pormenores todos "details all"
todos los "all the"
tiempo de "time of"
de expedición "of expedition"
expedición su "expedition his"

The obtained trigrams are the following:

ocupaba doctor el "engaged dr. the"
ocupaba doctor ferguson "engaged dr. ferguson"
ocupaba hacía tiempo "engaged ago time"
hacía tiempo mucho "ago time long"
hacía tiempo de "ago time upon"
hacía tiempo de "ago time of"
tiempo de pormenores "time upon details"
de pormenores todos "upon details all"
pormenores todos los "detail all the"
tiempo de expedición "time of expedition"
de expedición su "of expedition his"

The number of the 4-grams is a little less:

ocupaba hacía tiempo mucho "engaged ago time long"
ocupaba hacía tiempo de "engaged ago time upon"[1]
ocupaba hacía tiempo de "engaged ago time of"
hacía tiempo de pormenores "ago time upon details"
hacía tiempo de expedición "ago time of expedition"
tiempo de pormenores todos "time upon details all"

---

[1] This n-gram is repeated because there are two different words *de* ("of" and "upon") in the sentence. This means that the frequency of this n-gram is equal to two in our example.

de pormenores todos los "upon details all the"
tiempo de expedición su "time of expedition his"

There are several 5-grams:

ocupaba hacía tiempo de pormenores "engaged ago time upon details"
ocupaba hacía tiempo de expedición "engaged ago time of expedition"
hacía tiempo de pormenores todos "ago time upon details all"
hacía tiempo de expedición su "ago time of expedition his"
tiempo de pormenores todos los "time upon details all the"

In this case, three 6-grams can also be obtained:

ocupaba hacía tiempo de expedición su "engaged ago time of expedition his"
ocupaba hacía tiempo de pormenores todos "engaged ago time upon details all"
hacía tiempo de pormenores todos los "ago time upon details all the"

And finally, there is only one 7-gram:

ocupaba hacía tiempo de pormenores todos los "engaged ago time upon details all the"

The methodology for obtaining continuous syntactic n-grams is the same for all languages. As we can see, it is true in the case of English and Spanish; moreover, dependency-based trees have the same structure for all languages.

8.4 Example of Continuous Syntactic n-grams in English

For the example in English, we use the Stanford parser[2] [15]. First, we present the output of the parser as generated by the program itself, and then, in Figs. 8.3 and 8.4, we illustrate the dependency-based tree using multilevel arrows. The depth of the syntax tree is an important concept: starting from the root of a sentence and moving down while following the syntactic path. The sentence in English is the following:

The wildest cheering resounded on all sides; the name of Ferguson was in every mouth.

The direct output of the parser consists of two parts. In the first part, the information is presented in terms of constituency grammars, where a greater indent of a line corresponds to a greater depth of each element. However, for our purposes, the second part of the output, where the information is presented in terms of dependency grammars, is of more interest; in this part, we can see the pairs of words and syntactic dependencies between them. From this second part, we can directly build a syntax tree, as shown in Figs. 8.3 and 8.4.

Note that in the automatic parser, various errors may occur. In the figures below, one type of such errors is marked with the dotted line, where the word *wildest* was

---

[2] Parser is a program that generates syntactic trees. The trees are usually based on formal grammars of various types.

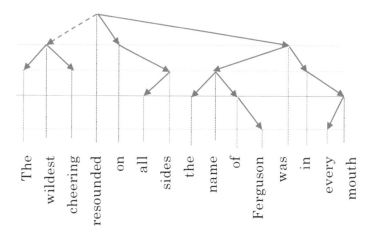

Fig. 8.3 Example of a syntax tree

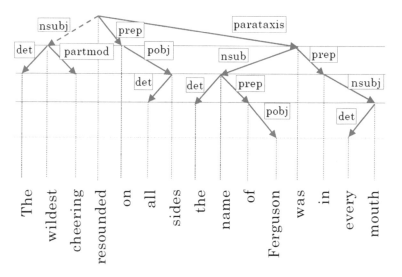

Fig. 8.4 Example of a syntax tree with tags

parsed as a noun and the word *cheering* as a participle; when the correct way would be to parse *cheering* as a noun and *wildest* as an adjective.

The first part of the output corresponds to the constituency formalism:

```
(ROOT
 (S
  (S
   (NP
    (NP (DT The) (NN wildest))
```

```
     (VP (VBG cheering)))
    (VP (VBD resounded)
     (PP (IN on)
      (NP (DT all) (NNS sides)))))
   (: ;)
   (S
    (S
     (NP
      (NP (DT the) (NN name))
      (PP (IN of)
       (NP (NNP Ferguson))))
     (VP (VBD was)
      (PP (IN in)
       (NP (DT every) (NN mouth)))))
 (. .)))
```

The second part of the output is presented in terms of dependency grammars:

```
det(wildest-2, The-1)
nsubj(resounded-4, wildest-2)
partmod(wildest-2, cheering-3)
root(ROOT-0, resounded-4)
prep(resounded-4, on-5)
det(sides-7, all-6)
pobj(on-5, sides-7)
det(name-10, the-9)
nsubj(was-13, name-10)
prep(name-10, of-11)
pobj(of-11, Ferguson-12)
parataxis(resounded-4, was-13)
prep(was-13, in-14)
det(mouth-16, every-15)
pobj(in-14, mouth-16)
```

One can see that for each pair of words, the parser indicates the type of the syntactic relation between them and the number of the word in the sentence. This information is important, because if a word is repeated in a sentence, there would be no way to determine to which of the two instances of that word the given pair refers.

The same syntax trees are shown in Figs. 8.3 and 8.4, the only difference is that in Fig. 8.4, the name of the corresponding syntactic dependency is shown above each arrow.

After the explanation above, it is quite obvious which n-grams can be obtained from this sentence.

For example, the following bigrams can be obtained:

resounded wildest
wildest cheering
wildest the
resounded on
on sides
resounded was
was name
name of
of Ferguson
was in
in mouth
mouth every

Also the following trigrams can be extracted:

resounded wildest the
resounded wildest cheering
resounded on sides
on sides all
resounded was name
resounded was in
was name the
was name of
name of ferguson
was in mouth
in mouth every

There are six 4-grams:

resounded on sides all
resounded was name the
resounded was name of
resounded was in mouth
was name of ferguson
was in mouth every

And finally, there are only two 5-grams:

resounded was name of ferguson
resounded was in mouth every

Chapter 9
Types of Syntactic n-grams According to their Components

9.1 n-grams of Lexical Elements

So, we have already learned how to obtain syntactic n-grams (although, at the moment, we are considering only continuous syntactic n-grams). Now let's discuss what types of syntactic n-grams exist depending on the elements they are formed of, i.e., what kind of elements (components) can be parts of syntactic n-grams. In fact, the considerations to be discussed are the same for any type of n-grams.

It is clear that the use of words is the most obvious option, as in all the examples mentioned above. It is also clear that instead of words we can use their normalized forms (lemmas), obtained by morphological normalization. Another similar option is to use the stems of words (the process of obtaining the stems is called stemming). In this sense, the lemma and the stem have the same function: they represent the entire set of grammatical forms that correspond to a word. The advantage of using morphological normalization is that the number of elements that can compose n-grams and, therefore, the number of n-grams are reduced, i.e., there are fewer dimensions in the vector space model.

9.2 n-grams of POS Tags

Similarly, instead of words we can use the grammatical information of each word (POS tag), for example, in the case of Spanish, we can use the tags that are produced by the parsers or morphological analyzers, as in the FreeLing system: NCFS000, VMII1S0, etc. The tags used in FreeLing are a de facto standard for encoding morphological information in Spanish; the standard is called EAGLES. In this case, the first letter corresponds to the grammatical class: "N" stands for noun, "V" for verb, etc. The second letter reflects a number of lexical properties, for example, in

© The Author(s), under exclusive license to Springer Nature Switzerland AG 2019   59
G. Sidorov, *Syntactic n-grams in Computational Linguistics*, SpringerBriefs
in Computer Science, https://doi.org/10.1007/978-3-030-14771-6_9

the case of nouns, "C" stands for common name (another value of this feature could be "P" – proper noun), etc. The subsequent letters reflect grammatical features, e.g., in the case of nouns, "F" corresponds to female gender, "M" to male gender, etc.

9.3   n-grams of Syntactic Relations Tags

In order to form syntactic n-grams, there is also an additional option of using new types of elements as compared to traditional n-grams: tags of syntactic relations (SR-tags) in a syntactic tree, for example, *nsubj* or *pobj* in the case of English (Fig. 8.4) or *espec* or *obj-prep* in the case of Spanish (Fig. 8.2). In this case, an n-gram would be a sequence of SR-tags, for example, *sp-mod obj-prep espec* (in the presented example, it is a trigram).

9.4   n-grams of Characters

The last option that exists for traditional n-grams construction is the use of characters as elements of n-grams. For example, in the phrase *John reads*, there are the following bigrams: "*jo*," "*oh*," "*hn*," "*n* ," " *r*," "*nr*," "*re*," "*ea*," "*ad*," and "*ds*." Here the space between the words is used as an element of the n-grams; one can also use punctuation marks. However, for some tasks, it is better not to consider auxiliary characters.

In the same way as in the case of traditional n-grams, one can also use characters as elements of syntactic n-grams; however, there is a need to obtain syntactic bigrams or trigrams of words in advance and then to consider the sequence of words in a syntactic n-gram as a source for constructing n-grams of characters. It is a matter of future research to determine whether this type of syntactic n-grams is useful. It turns out that the application of traditional n-grams of characters gives the best results in certain tasks, for example, in the task of authorship attribution [102]. However, in our point of view, the application of n-grams of characters is somewhat counter-intuitive, and it is necessary to analyze the reasons of its good performance (see the section concerning filtered n-grams of characters below).

9.5   Mixed n-grams

Finally, mixed n-grams may exist, which means that some elements of an n-gram are of a certain type, while other elements of the same n-gram are of another type. It seems that characters cannot be used in the mixed n-grams construction, as they are of a different nature: characters represent parts of words, while other types of elements represent words.

Concerning the mixed n-grams, it should be analyzed in the future, which combinations of elements (words, POS tags, SR-tags) in which positions (in the beginning, in the middle, or in the end of an n-gram) give better results.

9.6   Classification of n-grams According to their Components

To sum up, we can say that there are syntactic n-grams of:

- Lexical elements (words, lemmas, or stems)
- Part-of-speech tags (POS tags)
- Tags of syntactic relations (SR-tags)
- Characters
- Mixed syntactic n-grams (combinations of the above)

In [82], the idea of weighting the relations between elements of a syntactic n-gram is mentioned. This idea does not seem directly applicable within the context of the vector space model, where n-grams are the features (dimensions). However, this idea can prove useful when calculating the weights of syntactic n-grams, apart from the traditional values of *tf-idf* measure.

Chapter 10
Continuous and Noncontinuous
Syntactic n-grams

10.1 Continuous Syntactic n-grams

In the previous chapters, we introduced the new concept of syntactic n-grams, i.e., n-grams obtained following paths in syntax trees.

As we show in the following chapters, syntactic n-grams can give better results than traditional n-grams in various NLP tasks. Note that syntactic n-grams can be applied in any tasks where traditional n-grams are used, because they allow the construction of the vector space. We will analyze their applicability for the task of authorship attribution.

The disadvantage of syntactic n-grams consists in the fact that previous syntactic processing is required for their construction, which takes some processing time; however, it is not a serious limitation. One more limitation is that for some languages, there are no existing automatic parsers; nevertheless, the parsers do exist for the more widely spoken languages such as Spanish or English.

The discussion that follows in this chapter addresses the comparison of continuous syntactic n-grams with non-continuous syntactic n-grams.

The sentence to be analyzed is the following[1]:

Tomé el pingajo en mis manos y le di un par de vueltas de mala gana (lit: *I took the scrap in my hands and gave it a pair of turns without enthusiasm*) "*I took the scrap in my hands and turned it a couple of times unwillingly.*"

The syntax tree of the sample sentence is shown in Figs. 10.1 and 10.2, using the dependency and constituency formalisms [31, 38, 98]. Note that the expression *de_mala_gana* (lit: *without enthusiasm*) is considered as one word.

All the syntactic n-grams considered in the previous chapters are continuous, regardless of the type of elements they are formed of. That means that syntactic path

---

[1] A sentence from one of the books by A. Conan-Doyle.

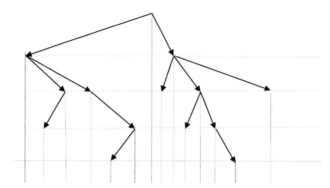

Tomé el pingajo en mis manos y le di un par de vueltas de_mala_gana

Fig. 10.1 Dependency-based tree. (Generated by the FreeLing parser)

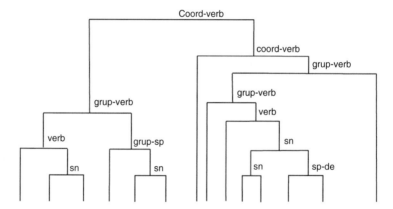

Tomé el pingajo en mis manos y le di un par de vueltas de_mala_gana

Fig. 10.2 Constituency-based tree. (Generated by the FreeLing parser)

we are following is never bifurcated. For example, in Fig. 10.3, the path marked with the bold arrows corresponds to the continuous syntactic 5-gram, *y di par de vueltas* (lit: and gave pair of turns).

We present another type of syntactic n-grams below, for which bifurcations are allowed.

10.2 Noncontinuous Syntactic n-grams

In this section, we present a generalization of the concept of continuous syntactic n-grams: non-continuous syntactic n-grams [97, 98].

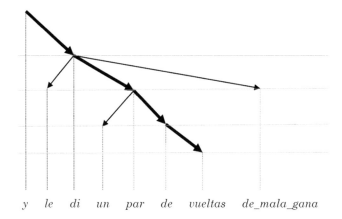

y   le   di   un   par   de   vueltas   de_mala_gana

Fig. 10.3 Continuous syntactic n-grams from the syntax tree fragment, a 5-gram

As shown in the previous section, the intuition behind the concept of continuous syntactic n-grams is mainly related to the fact that a sequence of related words can be considered as such, as a whole.

However, there are other interesting linguistic concepts that do not fit into the model of a one-dimensional sequence, for example, *verb valency patterns.*

For instance, the verb *to buy* has the following actants: *who, what, from who*, and *for how much money.* It would be interesting to have them presented in an n-gram at the same time.

However, both in the case of traditional n-grams and continuous syntactic n-grams, all these components would be separated into different n-grams. Thus, the intuition behind the concept of non-continuous syntactic n-grams is precisely the intention to merge semantically related words, even though they do not have a continuous path, but a path that connects them.

It is very easy to give a formal definition of non-continuous syntactic n-grams: these are all the sub-trees of length *n* of a syntax tree.

Two examples of non-continuous syntactic n-grams that are fragments of the sentence considered above are shown in Figs. 10.4 and 10.5. The n-grams are marked with the bold arrows.

In the first case (Fig. 10.4), the 5-gram is *y di par [un, de]* "and gave pair [a, of]." Note that it is necessary to introduce a metalanguage for the representation of non-continuous syntactic n-grams in order to resolve the ambiguity. The metalanguage is discussed in the next chapter.

In the second case (Fig. 10.5), the 5-gram is *y di [le, par, de_mala_gana]* "and gave [it, pair, without_enthusiasm]."

Thus, in a formal way, continuous syntactic n-grams are defined as all the sub-trees of length *n* without bifurcations of a syntax tree. Another way to put it formally is that each node of the path is connected to a single node.

Applying the proposed definitions, it follows that continuous syntactic n-grams are a particular case of non-continuous syntactic n-grams. The length of a tree is the

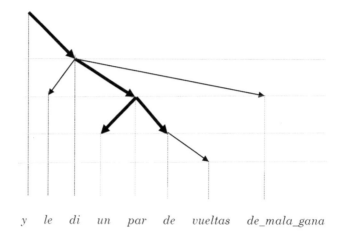

y   le   di   un   par   de   vueltas   de_mala_gana

Fig. 10.4 Non-continuous syntactic n-grams from the syntax tree fragment, a 5-gram

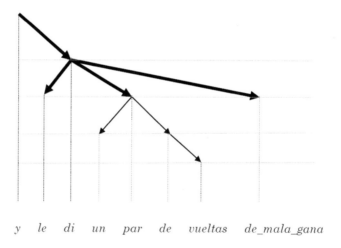

y   le   di   un   par   de   vueltas   de_mala_gana

Fig. 10.5 Non-continuous syntactic n-grams from the syntax tree fragment, another 5-gram

number of branches in this tree, which corresponds to the value of *n* (in the case of n-grams).

Another term that we propose in order to denote the non-continuous syntactic n-grams is t-n-grams (tree n-grams), i.e., n-grams of trees. There is also an option to use the term "arboreal n-gram." A. Gelbukh suggestion is to use the term "tree grams, t-grams"; however, in our opinion, the term "tree n-grams" seems more justified, since, in this way, there is a relation established between the proposed term and the traditional concept of n-grams. A consideration in favor of the term "t-gram" is its simple form; however, we prefer to adhere to the term "syntactic n-gram."

It is a matter of future work to determine the application of which type of n-grams (continuous or non-continuous) is more suitable for which computational linguistics tasks. It is possible that one type of n-grams is better for some tasks, while the other is better for other tasks.

It is noteworthy that the number of non-continuous syntactic n-grams is greater than the number of continuous syntactic n-grams, since the latter is a particular case of the former.

The construction algorithm (or the algorithm for obtaining) of continuous syntactic n-grams is relatively simple. For the root node, all the possible combinations of its children, whose size is not greater than n, are to be considered; this procedure should be repeated recursively for each child node. In this way, we are to go successively through all the nodes of a syntax tree.

Chapter 11
Metalanguage of Syntactic n-gram Representation

The question arises, how to represent non-continuous syntactic n-grams without resorting to their graphic form? Recall that continuous syntactic n-grams are simply sequences of words (obtained by following paths in a syntactic tree), but the case of the non-continuous syntactic n-gram is rather different.

We propose to use the following conventions. Note that these are conventions, so they can be modified in the future. Within each non-continuous syntactic n-gram, there may be continuous parts and one or several bifurcations. Let's separate the continuous elements of n-grams with whitespaces and put commas in the bifurcation parts; we will also use parentheses to mark the bifurcation parts in order to avoid the structural ambiguity in the future.

Note that we have always considered the highest level element to appear on the left side (the main word of the relation), and the component of the lower level on the right side (the word dependent on the syntactic relation). It is the most natural way; nevertheless, it is necessary to mention it explicitly.

Two examples of the non-continuous syntactic 5-grams are shown in Figs. 10.4 and 10.5, *y di par [un, de]* "and gave pair [a, of]"; *y di [le, par, de_mala_gana]* "and gave [it, pair, without_enthusiasm]."

Note that we cannot avoid using the brackets or commas in our metalanguage, as otherwise it becomes ambiguous. In our examples, it seems that we can avoid using the brackets if the comma indicates that the previous word is a part of a bifurcation. It is only possible when the elements in the bifurcation do not contain a path. For example, in the 5-gram, *y di [par un, de_mala_gana]* "and gave [pair a, without_enthusiasm]," the word *un* "a" is a dependent of *par* "pair," which is expressed with the whitespace; however, in this case, it is clear that we cannot avoid the brackets.

It is noteworthy that the brackets and the commas are parts of the n-grams now; however, this in no way precludes the possibility to identify the similarity between syntactic n-grams. Although they now contain some additional symbols and not only words, they can still be compared without any complications.

G. Sidorov, *Syntactic n-grams in Computational Linguistics*, SpringerBriefs in Computer Science, https://doi.org/10.1007/978-3-030-14771-6_11

Fig. 11.1 Example of a
possible ambiguity in
bifurcations

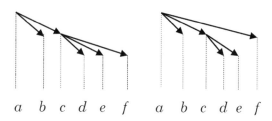

Here is another example of a possible ambiguity. Let's consider the case in which an n-gram has two bifurcations and multiple contiguous fragments. For example, the n-grams "*a [b, c [d, e, f]]*" and "*a [b, c [d, e], f]*" have a node *f* as the third node below the node *c*, or as the third node below the node *a*, see Fig. 11.1.

Now, there are two ways to tackle the bifurcation parts, i.e., the parts separated by commas:

1. As they appear in the text, which is the most natural way
2. To sort them in a certain way, for example, alphabetically, which decreases the number of n-grams

The latter option allows us to take into account the changes related to the word order. However, further research is required in order to determine which of the two options is better and for which NLP tasks.

Another possibility that we would like to mention is to mark the depth directly in the non-continuous syntactic n-grams. The intuition behind this idea is that, for some types of non-continuous syntactic n-grams, the position in the syntax tree of a sentence can be important. In this case, the notation would be: y_1 di_2 par_3 $[un_4, de_4]$ "and$_1$ gave$_2$ pair$_3$ [of$_4$, a$_4$]," y_1 di_2 $[le_3, par_3, de\_mala\_gana_3]$ "and$_1$ gave$_2$ [it$_3$, pair$_3$, without_enthusiasm$_3$]." Technically, it would be sufficient to mark the level of the first word only; we can mark the other levels as well, but it is not strictly necessary.

Note that this notation can also be used to denote the structure of an n-gram by replacing commas and brackets. It has to be taken into account that all the n-grams should originate from the level "1," regardless of their actual level in a sentence, since in the opposite case, it will not be possible to identify the similar n-grams that belong to different levels. Considering this complication in the n-gram construction, we tend to use brackets and commas.

We consider two examples of non-continuous syntactic n-gram construction below, one for Spanish and another for English, and compare them with continuous syntactic n-grams.

Chapter 12
Examples of Construction of Non-continuous Syntactic n-grams

12.1 Example for Spanish

In this section, we provide examples of the continuous and non-continuous syntactic n-gram construction for Spanish. We analyze the sample sentence provided in the previous chapter:

Tomé el pingajo en mis manos y le di un par de vueltas de mala gana (lit: *I took the scrap in my hands and gave it a pair of turns without enthusiasm*) '*I took the scrap in my hands and turned it a couple of times unwillingly.*'

In order to construct syntactic n-grams automatically, it is necessary to parse the text beforehand using a parser. For the Spanish language, we use the FreeLing parser [10, 80, 81], which is freely available online.

The parser can generate syntax trees in terms of two formats: constituency and dependency. The dependency-based tree is shown in Fig. 10.1 and the constituency-based in Fig. 10.2. Both formats have essentially the same information on words relations. For the syntactic n-gram construction, it seems better to use the dependency format, since this representation is more transparent. However, one can use the constituency-based tree in the same way.

It is noteworthy that the parser performs morphological analysis and lemmatization in the first place. As can be seen, a lemma and grammatical information correspond to each word in the sentence, e.g., *Tomé tomar* VMIS1S0 "Took take VMIS1S0." First comes the word, then the lemma, and finally the grammatical information.

We have already mentioned that in order to represent the grammatical information, the EAGLES coding scheme is applied, which is a de facto standard for the automatic morphological analysis of Spanish. For example, considering the VMIS1S0 tag, the first letter "V" stands for verb ("N" for noun, "A" for adjective, etc.), "I" stands for indicative, "S" for past, "1" for first person, and the other letter

G. Sidorov, *Syntactic n-grams in Computational Linguistics*, SpringerBriefs in Computer Science, https://doi.org/10.1007/978-3-030-14771-6_12

"S" for singular. As can be seen, each position encodes a specific type of grammatical information, and each tag contains at most seven positions, some of which may not be used in certain cases, for example, in the case of nouns.

First, we present the results of the parsing of the sentence above using the constituency formalism (Fig. 10.2).

```
+ coor-VB_[
  grup-verb_[
    +verb_[
      +(Tomé tomar VMIS1S0 -)
    ]
    sn_[
      espec-ms_[
        +j-ms_[
          +(el el DA0MS0 -)
        ]
      ]
      + grup-nom-ms_[
        +n-ms_[
          +(pingajo pingajo NCMS000 -)
        ]
      ]
    ]
    grup-sp_[
      +prep_[
        +(en en SPS00-)
      ]
      sn_[
        espec-fp_[
          +pos-fp_[
            +(mis mi DP1CPS -)
          ]
        ]
        +grup-nom-fp_[
          +n-fp_[
            +(manos mano NCFP000 -)
          ]
        ]
      ]
    ]
  ]
  +(y y CC -)
  grup-verb_[
    patons_[
      +paton-s_[
```

```
      +(le le PP3CSD00 -)
    ]
  ]
  +grup-verb_[
    +verb_[
      +(di dar VMIS1S0 -)
    ]
  ]
  sn_[
    espec-ms_[
      +indef-ms_[
        +(un uno DI0MS0 -)
      ]
    ]
    +grup-nom-ms_[
      +n-ms_[
        +(par par NCMS000 -)
      ]
    ]
    sp-de_[
      +(de de SPS00 -)
      sn_[
        +grup-nom-fp_[
          + n-fp_[
            +(vueltas vuelta NCFP000 -)
          ]
        ]
      ]
    ]
  ]
  sadv_[
    +(de_mala_gana de_mala_gana RG -)
  ]
]
F-term_[
  +(..Fp -)
]
]
```

Similar information is presented using the dependency formalism (Fig. 10.1).

```
coor-vb/top/(y y CC -) [
  grup-verb/co-v/(Tomé tomar VMIS1S0 -) [
    sn/dobj/(pingajo pingajo NCMS000 -) [
      espec-ms/espec/(el el DA0MS0 -)
    ]
```

```
  grup-sp/sp-obj/(en en SPS00 -) [
    sn/obj-prep/(manos mano NCFP000 -) [
      espec-fp/espec/(mis mi DP1CPS -)
    ]
  ]
]
grup-verb/co-v/(di dar VMIS1S0 -) [
  patons/iobj/(le le PP3CSD00 -)
  sn/dobj/(par par NCMS000 -) [
    espec-ms/espec/(un uno DI0MS0 -)
    sp-de/sp-mod/(de de SPS00 - ) [
      sn/obj-prep/(vueltas vuelta NCFP000 -)
    ]
  ]
  sadv/cc/(de_mala_gana de_mala_gana RG -)
]
F-term/modnomatch/(..Fp -)
]
```

As mentioned above, it is easier to use dependencies, because in this case, they practically contain syntactic n-grams.

It can be seen that the three words *de_mala_gana* (lit: without enthusiasm) actually represent a single adverb.

Now, let's present the extracted syntactic n-grams. First, we present the continuous syntactic n-grams.

The syntactic bigrams (basically, there is no difference between continuous and non-continuous bigrams) are:*y tomé* "and took"
tomé pingajo "took scrap"
pingajo el "scrap the"
tomé en "took in"
en manos "in hands"
manos mis "hands my"
y di "and gave"
di le "gave it"
di par "gave pair"
par un "pair a"
par de "pair of"
de vueltas "of turns"
di de_mala_gana "gave without_enthusiasm"

The continuous trigrams are:*y tomé pingajo* "and took scrap"
y tomé en "and took in"
tomé pingajo el "took scrap the"
tomé en manos "took in hands"
en manos mis "en hands my"
y di le "and gave it"
y di par "and gave pair"

y di de_mala_gana "and gave without_enthusiasm"
di par un "gave pair a"
di par de "gave pair of"
par de vueltas "pair of turns"

The continuous 4-grams are:*y tomé pingajo el* "and took scrap the"
y tomé en manos "and took in hands"
tomé en manos mis "took in hands my"
y di par un "and gave pair a"
y di par de "and gave pair of"
di par de vueltas "gave pair of turns"

We present the non-continuous syntactic n-grams without repeating the same elements (continuous n-grams), although they are also a part of the non-continuous syntactic n-grams. Note that in this case, we have to use the proposed notation for the non-continuous n-grams in order to be able to distinguish them from other possible configurations. The notation forms a part of the n-grams; it is the n-gram itself (not something additional). Thus, the new non-continuous trigrams (compared to the continuous n-grams) are:*tomé [pingajo en]* "took [scrap in]"
di [le par] "gave [it pair]"
di [le de_mala_gana] "gave [it without_enthusiasm]"
di [par de_mala_gana] "gave [pair without_enthusiasm]"
par [un de] "pair [a of]

The new non-continuous 4-grams are:*tomé [pingajo el, en]* "took [scrap the, in]"
tomé [pingajo, en manos] "took [scrap, in hands]"
di [le, par un] "gave [it, pair a]"
di [le, par de] "gave [it, pair of]"
di [le, par, de_mala_gana] "gave [it, pair, without_enthusiasm]"
di [par un, de_mala_gana] "gave [pair a, without_enthusiasm]"
di [par de, de_mala_gana] 'gave [pair of, without_enthusiasm]'
par [un, de vueltas] "pair [a, of turns]"

12.2 Example for English

In this section, we discuss the construction of syntactic n-grams for the English language. To simplify the comparison with Spanish, we consider the translation of the sentence provided in the previous section. Note that in this case, the figure that corresponds to the tree has been generated automatically; the code, which allows it, is freely available on the author's personal web page[1].

I took the scrap in my hands and turned it a couple of times unwillingly.

One can use the same parser as in the previous examples, i.e., FreeLing; however, let's try to use another parser for English that we have already mentioned before – the Stanford parser [15]. The constituency-based tree is shown in Fig. 12.1.

---

[1] http://www.cic.ipn.mx/~sidorov

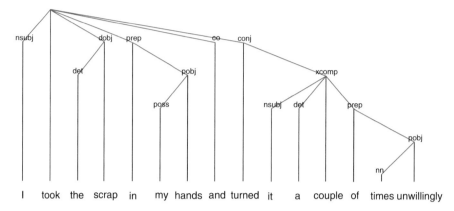

Fig. 12.1 Constituency-based tree for the example in English

As mentioned above, most parsers generate their output in both dependency and constituency formalisms. The output in terms of constituency grammars is the following:

```
(ROOT
  (S
    (NP (PRP I))
    (VP
      (VP (VBD took)
        (NP (DT the) (NN scrap))
        (PP (IN in)
          (NP (PRP $ my) (NNS hands))))
      (CC and)
      (VP (VBD turned)
        (S
          (NP (PRP it))
          (NP
            (NP (DT a) (NN couple))
            (PP (IN of)
              (NP (NNS times) (NN unwillingly)))))))
    (..)))
```

As we have already discussed, in the Stanford parser, a very simple but expressive representation of a dependency-based tree is used: relation name and two words – or their POS tags or lemmas, depending on the type of elements we want to consider – along with the corresponding numbers of their positions in a sentence. The main word is mentioned first, and then the dependent word, i.e., the order of the words is important. This information allows building the syntax tree in a unique way. The following is the output of the parser in the format mentioned above.

```
nsubj(took-2, I-1)
root(ROOT-0, took-2)
det(scrap-4, the-3)
dobj(took-2, scrap-4)
prep(took-2, in-5)
poss(hands-7, my-6)
pobj(in-5, hands-7)
cc(took-2, and-8)
conj(took-2, turned-9)
nsubj(couple-12, it-10)
det(couple-12, a-11)
xcomp(turned-9, 12-couple)
prep(couple-12, of-13)
nn(unwillingly-15, times-14)
pobj(of-13, unwillingly-15)
```

It can be seen that although the sentence is very similar to the one above, the other parser applied different rules, to be more precise, handled the conjunction in a different way and also committed some errors: for example, the word *unwillingly* was incorrectly related to *of* instead of *turned*; the word *it* was related to *couple* and not to *turned*. However, the parser errors do not conceptually affect our discussion, since our task is not to improve the parser but to apply existing tools. It is also worth mentioning that eventually the parsers are improving. Another interesting consideration that has been already mentioned is that parser errors are usually related to various types of syntactic ambiguity.

Now we proceed to the construction of continuous and non-continuous syntactic n-grams. Syntactic bigrams – recall that in principle, there is no difference between continuous and non-continuous syntactic bigrams – are as follows:*took I*
took scrap
scrap the
took in
in hands
hands my
took and
took turned
turned couple
couple it
couple a
couple of
of unwillingly
unwillingly times

The continuous syntactic trigrams are:*took scrap the*
took in hands
in hands my
took turned couple
turned couple it
couple turned a

turned couple of
couple of unwillingly
of unwillingly times

The continuous syntactic 4-grams are:*took in hands my*
took turned couple it
took turned couple a
took turned couple of
turned couple of unwillingly
couple of unwillingly times

As in the previous example, we do not repeat the same elements, although the continuous syntactic n-grams are also a part of the non-continuous syntactic n-grams.

The non-continuous syntactic trigrams – the new ones (some of them may be parser errors; however, it does not affect the proposed idea, as these are errors of another type and can be corrected by improving the parser itself) – are:*took [I, scrap]*
took [I, in]
took [I, and]
took [I, turned]
took [scrap, in]
took [scrap, and]
took [scrap, turned]
took [in, and]
took [in, turned]
took [and, turned]
couple [it, a]
couple [it, of]
couple [a, of]

The non-continuous 4-grams (the new ones) are:*took [I, scrap the]*
took [in, scrap the]
took [and, scrap the]
took [turned, scrap the]
took [I, in hands]
took [scrap, in hands]
took [and, in hands]
took [turned, in hands]
took [I, scrap, in]
took [I, scrap, and]
took [I, scrap, turned]
took [scrap, in, and]
took [scrap, in, turned]
took [in, and, turned]
couple [it, a, of]
couple [it, of unwillingly]
couple [a, of unwillingly]

Note that in this case, we took the elements of the non-continuous syntactic n-grams in the order of their appearance in the text. As mentioned above, another option is to sort them in some way, for example, alphabetically.

Chapter 13
Automatic Analysis of Authorship Using Syntactic n-grams

13.1 Corpus Preparation for the Automatic Authorship Attribution Task

We have conducted various experiments [93] in order to test the usefulness of the concept of syntactic n-grams. Essentially, we consider the task of authorship attribution, i.e., there are texts for which the authors are known and a text for which we have to determine the author (among the considered authors only). In our case, we use a corpus composed of texts written by three different authors.

The task of authorship attribution is clearly a classification task: the authors correspond to the names of the classes, the classes are the texts for which the authors are known, and the task is based on the decision to which class a text belongs [4, 52, 57, 102]. The features that we use are traditional n-grams and syntactic n-grams ranging in size from two to five. We also employ a tool that makes it easy to apply various available classification algorithms: the WEKA system [45].

We use a corpus composed of works by the following authors: Booth Tarkington, George Vaizey, and Louis Tracy (the authors wrote in English in the nineteenth century). The composed corpus contains five novels by each author for training, in total 11 MB, and three works by each author for classification, in total 6 MB [93–95]. The Stanford parser is used to obtain the syntactic n-grams.

13.2 Evaluation of the Authorship Attribution Task Using Syntactic n-grams

For the design of experiments, we use profiles of various sizes. The term "profile" means that we use the corresponding number of the most frequent n-grams, for example, for the profile of 400, we use 400 n-grams with greater frequency in the training corpus, etc.

© The Author(s), under exclusive license to Springer Nature Switzerland AG 2019   79
G. Sidorov, *Syntactic n-grams in Computational Linguistics*, SpringerBriefs
in Computer Science, https://doi.org/10.1007/978-3-030-14771-6_13

We apply a standard classification algorithm called "support vector machine" (SVM). It is known that for many tasks, the support vector machine algorithm outperforms other classification algorithms.

Classification results (for the authorship attribution task) for bigrams are shown in Table 13.1, and for trigrams in Table 13.2. To compare the results, we apply other ways of features selection: n-grams of words, n-grams of POS tags, and n-grams of characters. The best results are underlined.

"ND" means that not many n-grams were found for the specific profile, i.e., the number of n-grams was relatively small.

As can be seen, the method based on syntactic n-grams gives the best results. However, it is noteworthy that the top line (facility of obtaining the results) for the considered problem is quite high, as we have a great amount of training data and use only three classes (authors). The detailed information on the experiments and the experimental data for a larger number of authors can be found in our previous studies [93–95], so we do not present the detailed description in this book.

Table 13.1 Results of the authorship attribution task for bigrams

Profile size	Syntactic n-grams of SR-tags	n-grams of POS tags	n-grams of characters	n-grams of words
400	100%	90%	90%	86%
1000	100%	95%	95%	86%
4000	100%	ND	90%	86%
7000	100%	ND	ND	86%
11,000	100%	ND	ND	89%

Table 13.2 Results of the authorship attribution task for trigrams

Profile size	Syntactic n-grams of SR-tags	n-grams of POS tags	n-grams of characters	n-grams of words
400	100%	90%	76%	81%
1000	100%	90%	86%	71%
4000	100%	100%	95%	95%
7000	100%	100%	90%	90%
11,000	100%	95%	100%	90%

Chapter 14
Filtered n-grams

14.1   Idea of Filtered n-grams

In this and the following chapters, we present two ideas related to the non-linear construction of n-grams. Recall that the non-linear construction consists in taking the elements which form n-grams in a different order than the surface (textual) representation, i.e., in a different way than words (lemmas, POS tags, etc.) appear in a text.

In the previous chapters, we discussed the concept of syntactic n-grams, where the order in which the words are taken is defined by a syntax tree.

Another option to obtain n-grams, in a different from taking the elements as they appear in a text way, is to filter out certain elements in a text. In this way, the words that are not neighbors can be considered as such.

In fact, in its simplest version, this idea can be widely applied – stop words are filtered out during the construction of n-grams.

What we propose in this chapter is to apply this idea consistently and to filter out words in texts using some criteria. The most obvious criterion is to use the *tf-idf* measure, which is discussed in detail in the first part of this book. However, one can apply other measures. Somewhat similar happens with the stop words whose *tf-idf* values are very low due to their low *idf*.

The next step is to choose a threshold in order to filter out the words. It is a matter of future experiments to determine the optimal thresholds. Note that we recommend considering not only one threshold to discard the upper or the lower part but a combination of two thresholds in order to discard the upper part and the lower parts simultaneously. This corresponds to the intuition that the most important values are in the middle. We can generalize this idea and use not only two thresholds but a series of pairs of thresholds, although it seems unlikely that there are specific optimal ranges for the values of the features.

© The Author(s), under exclusive license to Springer Nature Switzerland AG 2019   81
G. Sidorov, *Syntactic n-grams in Computational Linguistics*, SpringerBriefs
in Computer Science, https://doi.org/10.1007/978-3-030-14771-6_14

Note that this idea can be easily combined with the idea of syntactic n-grams: we just skip the filtered words according to the selected thresholds in our path in a syntax tree. In this case, an interesting question arises, what is to be done in the case of bifurcations? We believe that we should follow all the possible paths that originate from a bifurcation, although we should not consider the word itself in this bifurcation.

14.2   Example of Filtered n-grams

Let's consider a simple example of the filtered n-gram construction. Let's assume that we are to analyze the sentence that has been already used as an example in the previous chapters.

Tomé el pingajo en mis manos y le di un par de vueltas de mala gana (lit: *I took the scrap in my hands and gave it a pair of turns without enthusiasm*) "*I took the scrap in my hands and turned it a couple of times unwillingly.*"

Suppose that we want to obtain traditional n-grams constructed out of the filtered words. We will present a table with the *tf-idf* values of each word in an imaginary collection, see Table 14.1.

Now, let's assume that we filter out the words with very high or very low *tf-idf* values. For example, we select the thresholds: (1) ">0.1" and (2) "<1.3." Only the words in bold *tomé* "took," *pingajo* "scrap," *par* "pair," and *vueltas* "turns" are in the considered range.

Table 14.1 Possible values of *tf-idf* of words

Word	*tf-idf*
manos "hands"	1.5
de_mala_gana "without_enthusiasm"	1.46
Upper threshold, <1.3	
vueltas **"turns"**	**1.23**
tomé **"took"**	**1.2**
par **"pair"**	**0.9**
pingajo **"scrap"**	**0.7**
Lower threshold, >0.1	
di "gave"	0.003
el "the"	0
en "in"	0
mis "my"	0
y "and"	0
le "it"	0
un "a"	0
de "of"	0

Note that the comparison signs of the thresholds can differ from our example, i.e., for the upper threshold, we use "less-than" (<) sign; one can try "greater-than" (>) sign and use the words above the threshold, and not the ones below, as in the example.

> Using the words that are still under consideration, we can construct the n-grams. For example, the traditional bigrams would be:*tomé pingajo* "took scrap"
> *pingajo manos* "scrap hands"
> *manos par* "hands pair"
> *par vueltas* "pair turns"
>
> The continuous syntactic bigrams would be:*tomé pingajo* "took scrap"
> *tomé manos* "took hands"
> *par vueltas* "pair turns"
>
> If we also consider non-continuous syntactic bigrams, the following bigram will be added:*[tomé, pingajo]* "[took, scrap]"

It is quite curious, because as we have stated above, continuous and non-continuous bigrams coincide. This situation changes when we start filtering out the elements of a syntax tree without deleting paths. To check how this latter bigram is constructed, please refer to Fig. 10.1. We start with the root, which is filtered out based on the thresholds. Since we are in a bifurcation, we mark it with brackets and then look for two unfiltered elements on each side of the bifurcation, which we separate by commas. It is noteworthy that a situation like this can only occur while constructing filtered n-grams.

14.3   Filtered n-grams of Characters

Another idea that we would like to present in this book is related to the non-linear construction of n-grams of characters. In this case, one option is to filter out the words in the first place – for example, using *tf- idf* – and then to construct the n-grams of characters out of the remaining words. This idea is similar to the one already discussed in this chapter.

However, there is another option, which consists in filtering out the characters before we start constructing n-grams out of them. Basically, the idea is to filter out the characters that occupy certain positions in words or have certain features.

More specifically, regarding the features, we can filter, for example, the vowels and construct n-grams out of the remaining characters. One can try several types of characters features for various tasks.

When it comes to the positions of characters, we can consider, for example, only the first three or the last three characters of each word and ignore (filter out) the remaining characters of the word. When dealing with the Spanish language, this filtering strategy should take into account affixes (suffixes, prefixes, inflexions) and assign less weight to the n-grams that represent the stems of words. It is worth mentioning that one can do the opposite: consider the n-grams of characters that correspond to the stems and try to discard the n-grams that are related to the grammatical elements.

It is known that n-grams of characters give good results in the task of authorship attribution, i.e., reflect the personal style. The reason for this is not entirely clear, and we believe that experiments with various strategies of the non-linear construction of n-grams of characters can clarify which lexical or grammatical phenomenon is behind this type of n-grams. It is necessary to perform experiments with various parameters and with various n-gram construction strategies.

Chapter 15
Generalized n-grams

15.1 Idea of Generalized n-grams

Another idea related to the non-linear construction of n-grams, i.e., using distinct elements or distinct order of their appearance in a text, is the idea of replacing words by their synonyms or by the generalized concepts that correspond to the words according to a certain ontology.

We will call this type of n-grams "generalized n-grams." Their construction is non-linear, because the n-grams are not constructed out of words according to their appearance in a text.

When replacing words by their synonyms, we are at the same ontology level, and when using their hypernyms, we are moving to a higher ontology level. In both situations, it is highly desirable to perform the word sense disambiguation task beforehand, since the selection of correct synonyms and hypernyms greatly depends on this task.

The general idea behind generalized n-grams is to reduce the lexical variety of texts, since in this way, the number of n-grams is substantially decreased. It is quite clear that this idea can be easily combined with the ideas of syntactic and filtered n-grams.

The application of information concerning synonyms is rather simple: for each word we compose the list of synonyms, e.g., we can use WordNet synsets or any thesaurus and replace the word by the first synonym in the list and then proceed to the n-grams construction.

There are several strategies for using hypernyms available in ontologies. We can always use the current level of each word plus a constant.

$$hypernym\_level = word\_level + c$$

In this case, we have to move c levels higher in the ontology we are using.

G. Sidorov, *Syntactic n-grams in Computational Linguistics*, SpringerBriefs
in Computer Science, https://doi.org/10.1007/978-3-030-14771-6_15

Another possibility is to set a reasonably low ontology level and always move up from this level. If we come across a word of a very high level, it is advisable to leave it alone and not to move down to the corresponding level.

In this way, we replace the words by their synonyms or hypernyms and then construct the n-grams out of these new elements.

15.2   Example of Generalized n-grams

The case of synonyms seems quite obvious. Let's consider an example of hypernyms.

Let's use the same sample sentence as in the previous chapter. Assume that we use the filtering strategy and remain with the following filtered words: *tomé* "took," *pingajo* "scrap," *manos* "hands," *par* "pair," *vueltas* "turns."

As an example we use the strategy of moving only one level up in the ontology.

Assume that we have the following hypernyms: *manos* "hands" → *brazos* "arms" (strictly speaking, it is a holonym; however, it serves our purpose), *tomé* "took" → *actué* "acted," *pingajo* "scrap" → *herramienta* "tool," *vuelta* "turn" → *movimiento* "movement," *par* "pair" → *número* "number." Obviously, this information depends on the specific ontology, where the words and correspondences are to be found.

Now we can construct the n-grams using generalized concepts and not words as such, e.g., the bigram *tomé pingajo* "took scrap" is replaced by *actué herramienta* "acted tool" or *actuar herramienta* "act tool." The usefulness of this replacement depends on our purposes. The advantage is that the words *martillo* "hammer," *cuchillo* "knife," etc. would have the same hypernym *herramienta* "tool"; in the same way, the words tomé "took," clavé "stabbed," corté "cut," etc. would have the hypernym *actúe* "acted" or *actuar* "to act."

It is a matter of future studies to determine the usefulness of generalized n-grams and the tasks for which their application would give better results than using the other types of n-grams.

Bibliography

1. Abbasi, A., Chen, H.: Applying authorship analysis to extremist-group web forum messages. IEEE Intelligent Systems, Vol. 20, No. 5, pp. 67–75 (2005)
2. Agarwal, A., Biads, F., Mckeown, K.R.: Contextual Phrase-Level Polarity Analysis using Lexical Affect Scoring and Syntactic N-grams. In: Proceedings of the 12th Conference of the European Chapter of the ACL (EACL), pp. 24–32 (2009)
3. Aguilar-Galicia, H., Sidorov, G., Ledeneva, Y.: Extracción automática de hechos de libros de texto basada en estructuras sintácticas [(in Spanish) Automatic extraction of facts in text books based on syntactic structures]. Research in computing science, Vol. 55, pp. 15–26 (2012)
4. Argamon, S., Juola, P.: Overview of the international authorship identification competition at PAN-2011. In: Proc. of 5th Int. Workshop on Uncovering Plagiarism, Authorship, and Social Software Misuse (2011)
5. Argamon, S., Whitelaw, C., Chase, P., Hota, S.R., Garg, N., Levitan, S.: Stylistic text classification using functional lexical features. Journal of the American Society of Information Science and Technology, Vol. 58, No. 6, pp. 802–822 (2007)
6. Baayen, H., Tweedie, F. and Halteren, H.: Outside The Cave of Shadows: Using Syntactic Annotation to Enhance Authorship Attribution. Literary and Linguistic Computing, pp. 121–131 (1996)
7. Baeza-Yates, R., Ribeiro-Neto, B.: Modern Information Retrieval. Addison-Wesley (1999)
8. Baroni, M., Lenci, A. Distributional memory: A general framework for corpus-based semantics. Computational Linguistics, 36(4):673–721 (2010)
9. Burrows, J.: Word-patterns and story-shapes: The statistical analysis of narrative style. Literary and Linguistic Computing. Vol. 2, No. 2, pp. 61–70 (1987)
10. Carreras, X., Chao, I., Padró, L., Padró, M.: FreeLing: An Open-Source Suite of Language Analyzers. In: Proceedings of the 4th International Conference on Language Resources and Evaluation (LREC'04) (2004)
11. Cazés Menache, D., del Castillo, N., Mansilla, R., Pineda, L.A., Sidorov, G., Sierra Martínez, G.: El dominio de la lingüística: más allá de las ciencias exactas y naturales. UNAM, 213 p. (2009)
12. Chen, W., Kazama, J., Uchimoto, K., Torisawa, K.: Improving dependency parsing with subtrees from auto-parsed data. In: EMNLP, pp. 570–579 (2009)
13. Cheng, W., Greaves, C., Warren, M.: From n-gram to skipgram to concgram. International Journal of Corpus Linguistics 11, no. 4, pp 411–433 (2006)

14. Daelemans, W.: Explanation in computational stylometry. In: Proceedings of the 14th International Conference on Intelligent Text Processing and Computational Linguistics, pp. 451–462 (2013)
15. de Marneffe, M.C., MacCartney, B., Manning, C.D.: Generating Typed Dependency Parses from Phrase Structure Parses. In: Proc. of LREC (2006)
16. Díaz Rangel, I., Sidorov, G., Suárez-Guerra, S.: Creación y evaluación de un diccionario marcado con emociones y ponderado para el español. Onomazein, 29 (2014)
17. Diederich, J., Kindermann, J., Leopold, E., Paass, G.: Authorship attribution with support vector machines. Applied Intelligence, Vol. 19, No. 1–2, pp. 109–123 (2003)
18. Dumais, S.T.: Latent Semantic Analysis. Annual Review of Information Science and Technology 38: 188 (2005)
19. Erk, K., Padó, S.: A structured vector space model for word meaning in context. In: Proceedings of EMNLP, pp. 897–906, Honolulu, HI (2008)
20. Erk, K., Padó, S., Padó, U.: A flexible, corpus-driven model of regular and inverse selectional preferences. Computational Linguistics, 36(4):723–763 (2010)
21. Feng, L., Jansche, M., Huenerfauth, M., Elhadad, N.: A comparison of features for automatic readability assessment. In: Proceedings of the 23rd International Conference on Computational Linguistics, pp. 276–284 (2010)
22. Fillmore, Ch., Langendoen, T. (eds): Studies in Linguistic Semantics. (1971)
23. Firth, J.R.: A Synopsis of Linguistic Theory. In: Palmer, F.R. (ed), (1968) Selected Papers of J.R. Firth 1952-59. London/Harlow: Longmans (1957)
24. Fucks, W.: On the mathematical analysis of style. Biometrica, Vol. 39, No. 1–2, pp. 122–129 (1952)
25. Gale, W.A., Church, K.W.: A program for aligning sentences in bilingual corpora. In: Proceedings of the 29th Annual Meeting of the Association for Computational Linguistics, Berkeley, California (1991)
26. Galitsky, B., Ilvovsky, D., Kuznetsov, S.O.: Detecting logical argumentation in text via communicative discourse tree. Journal of Experimental & Theoretical Artificial Intelligence, 30(5):637–663 (2018)
27. Galitsky, B.A.: Matching parse thickets for open domain question answering. Data and Knowledge Engineering 107:24–50 (2017)
28. Galitsky, B.A., Ilvovsky, D.I., Kuznetsov, S.O: Rhetoric Map of an Answer to Compound Queries. In: ACL (2), pp. 681–686 (2015)
29. Galitsky, B.A., Kuznetsov, S.O., Usikov, D.: Parse Thicket Representation for Multi-sentence Search. In: Proc. Int. Conf. on Conceptual Structures (ICCS 2013), LNCS 7735, pp. 153–172 (2013)
30. Gelbukh, A., Alexandrov, M., Han, SangYong: Detecting Inflection Patterns in Natural Language by Minimization of Morphological Model. In: A. Sanfeliu, J.F. Martínez, Trinidad, J.A. Carrasco Ochoa (Eds.) Lecture Notes in Computer Science N 3287, Springer-Verlag, pp. 432–438 (2004)
31. Gelbukh, A., Calvo, H., Torres, S.: Transforming a Constituency Treebank into a Dependency Treebank. Procesamiento de Lenguaje Natural, No 35. Sociedad Española para el Procesamiento de Lenguaje Natural (SEPLN) (2005)
32. Gelbukh, A., Sidorov, G.: Procesamiento automático del español con enfoque en recursos léxicos grandes. IPN, 307 p. (2010)
33. Gelbukh, A., Sidorov, G.: Approach to construction of automatic morphological analysis systems for inflective languages with little effort. Lecture Notes in Computer Science, N 2588, Springer-Verlag, pp. 215–220 (2003)
34. Gelbukh, A., Sidorov, G.: Zipf and Heaps Laws' Coefficients Depend on Language. Lecture Notes in Computer Science N 2004, Sringer-Verlag, pp. 330–333 (2001)
35. Gelbukh A., Sidorov, G.: Alignment of Paragraphs in Bilingual Texts using Bilingual Dictionaries and Dynamic Programming. Lecture Notes in Computer Science, N 4225, Springer-Verlag, pp 824-833 (2006)

36. Gelbukh, A., Sidorov, G., Guzman-Arenas, A.: Use of a weighted topic hierarchy for text retrieval and classification. Lecture Notes in Artificial Intelligence, No. 1692, Springer, pp. 130–135 (1999)
37. Gelbukh, A., Sidorov, G., Han, SangYong: On Some Optimization Heuristics for Lesk-Like WSD Algorithms. Lecture Notes in Computer Science, N 3513, Springer-Verlag, pp. 402–405 (2005)
38. Gelbukh, A., Sidorov, G., Han, SangYong, Hernández-Rubio, E.: Automatic Enrichment of Very Large Dictionary of Word Combinations on the Basis of Dependency Formalism. Lecture Notes in Artificial Intelligence N 2972, Springer-Verlag, pp 430-437 (2004)
39. Goldberg, Y: A Primer on Neural Network Models for Natural Language Processing. Journal of Artificial Intelligence Research 57:345–420 (2016)
40. Goldberg, Y., Orwant, J.: A Dataset of Syntactic-Ngrams over Time from a Very Large Corpus of English Books. In: Proc. of Second Joint Conference on Lexical and Computational Semantics (*SEM), Volume 1: Proceedings of the Main Conference and the Shared Task, pp. 241–247, Atlanta, Georgia (2013)
41. Goldsmith, J.: Unsupervised Learning of the Morphology of a Natural Language. Computational Linguistics 27:2, 153–198 (2001)
42. Gómez-Adorno, H., Sidorov, G., Pinto, D., Markov, I.: A graph based authorship identification approach. Working Notes Papers of the CLEF 2015 Evaluation Labs, Vol. 1391 (2015)
43. Grieve, J.: Quantitative authorship attribution: A history and an evaluation of techniques. MSc dis. Simon Fraser University (2005)
44. Habash, N.: The Use of a Structural N-gram Language Model in Generation-Heavy Hybrid Machine Translation. LNCS, 3123, pp. 61–69 (2004)
45. Hall, M., Frank, E., Holmes, G., Pfahringer, B., Reutemann, P., Witten, I.H.: The WEKA Data Mining Software: An Update; SIGKDD Explorations, 11(1), pp. 10–18 (2009)
46. Hernández-Reyes, E., Martínez-Trinidad, J. Fco., Carrasco-Ochoa, J.A., García-Hernández, R.A.: Document Representation Based on Maximal Frequent Sequence Sets. LNCS 4225, pp. 854–863 (2006)
47. Hinton, G.E., Srivastava, N., Krizhevsky, A., Sutskever, I., Salakhutdinov, R.R.: Improving neural networks by preventing co-adaptation of feature detectors. arXiv:1207.0580 (2012)
48. Holmes, D.: Authorship attribution. Computers and the Humanities. Vol. 28, No. 2, pp. 87–106 (1994)
49. Inteligencia Artificial. G. Sidorov (Ed.), Alfa Omega (2018)
50. Jarvis, S., Bestgen, Y., Pepper, S.: Maximizing classification accuracy in native language identification. In: Proceeding of the 8th Workshop on Innovative Use of NLP for Building Educational Applications, pp. 111–118 (2013)
51. Jiménez-Salazar, H., Pinto, D., Rosso, P.: Uso del punto de transición en la selección de términos índice para agrupamiento de textos cortos. Procesamiento del Lenguaje Natural, 35, pp. 383–390 (2005)
52. Juola, P.: Authorship Attribution. Foundations and Trends in Information Retrieval. 1(3):233–334 (2006)
53. Jurafsky, D., Martin, J.: Speech and Language Processing. Prentice Hall (2009)
54. Kay, M., Roscheisen, M.: Text-translation alignment. Computational Linguistics, 19(1):121–142 (1993)
55. Kestemont, M.: Function words in authorship attribution. From black magic to theory? In: Proceedings of the 3rd Workshop on Computational Linguistics for Literature, pp. 59–66 (2014)
56. Khalilov, M., Fonollosa, J.A.R.: N-gram-based Statistical Machine Translation versus Syntax Augmented Machine Translation: comparison and system combination. In: Proceedings of the 12th Conference of the European Chapter of the ACL, pp. 424–432 (2009)
57. Koppel, M., Schler, J., Argamon, S.: Authorship attribution in the wild. Language Resources and Evaluation 45(1):83–94 (2011)

58. Koppel, M., Winter, Y.: Determining if two documents are written by the same author. Journal of the American Society for Information Science and Technology. Vol. 65, No. 1, pp. 178–187 (2014)
59. LeCun, Y., Bengio, Y., Hinton, G.: Deep learning. Nature, Vol. 521, 436–445 (2015)
60. LeCun, Y., Bottou, L., Orr, G., Muller, K.: Efficient BackProp. In: Neural Networks: Tricks of the trade. Springer (1998)
61. Lesk, M. Automatic sense disambiguation using machine readable dictionaries: how to tell a pine cone from an ice cream cone. Proc. of ACM SIGDOC Conference, Toronto, Canada, pp. 24-26 (1986)
62. Lewis, D.D., Yang, Y., Rose, T.G., Li, F.: RCV1: A new benchmark collection for text categorization research. Journal of Machine Learning Research, Vol. 5, pp. 361–397 (2004)
63. Lin, D.: Automatic retrieval and clustering of similar words. Proceedings of the 36th Annual Meeting of the Association for Computational Linguistics and 17th International Conference on Computational Linguistics - Volume 2, ACL '98, pp. 768–774, Stroudsburg, PA, USA (1998)
64. Lin, D., Pantel, P.: Dirt: discovery of inference rules from text. KDD, pp. 323–328 (2001)
65. Luyckx K., Daelemans W. Authorship attribution and verification with many authors and limited data. In: Proceedings of the 22nd International Conference on Computational Linguistics, pp. 513–520 (2008)
66. Manning, C., Schütze, H.: Foundations of Statistical Natural Language Processing. MIT Press, Cambridge, MA (1999)
67. Markov, I., Baptista, J., Pichardo-Lagunas, O.: Authorship attribution in Portuguese using character n-grams. Acta Polytechnica Hungarica, Vol. 14, No. 3, pp. 59–78 (2017)
68. Markov, I., Gómez-Adorno, H., Posadas-Durán, J.-P., Sidorov, G., Gelbukh, A.: Author profiling with doc2vec neural network-based document embeddings. In: Proceedings of the 15th Mexican International Conference on Artificial Intelligence, LNAI, Vol. 10062, pp. 117–131 (2017)
69. Markov, I., Gómez-Adorno, H., Sidorov, G.: Language- and subtask-dependent feature selection and classifier parameter tuning for author profiling. Working Notes Papers of the CLEF 2017 Evaluation Labs, Vol. 1866 (2017)
70. Markov, I., Stamatatos, E., Sidorov, G.: Improving cross-topic authorship attribution: The role of pre-processing. In: Proceedings of the 18th International Conference on Computational Linguistics and Intelligent Text Processing (2017)
71. McNamara, D., Louwerse, M., McCarthy, P., Graesser, A.: Cohmetrix: Capturing linguistic features of cohesion. Discourse Processes, Vol. 47, No. 4, pp. 292–330 (2010)
72. Medina Urrea, A.: Automatic Discovery of Affixes by means of a Corpus: A Catalog of Spanish Affixes. Journal of Quantitative Linguistics 7(2), pp. 97–114 (2000)
73. Mendenhall, T.: The characteristic curves of composition. Science, Vol. 9, No. 214, pp. 237–249 (1887)
74. Mikolov, T., Chen, K., Corrado, G., Dean, J.: Efficient Estimation of Word Representations in Vector Space. arXiv:1301.3781 (2013)
75. Mikolov, T., Sutskever, I., Chen, K., Corrado, G.S., Dean, J.: Distributed Representations of Words and Phrases and their Compositionality. In: Burges, C.J.C., Bottou, L., Welling, M., Ghahramani, Z., Weinberger, K.Q. (Eds.), Advances in Neural Information Processing Systems 26, pp. 3111–3119 (2013)
76. Miranda-Jimenez, S., Gelbukh, A., Sidorov, G: Generación de resúmenes por medio de síntesis de grafos conceptuales. Revista "SIGNOS. Estudios de Lingüística", 47(86) (2014)
77. Montes y Gómez, M., Gelbukh, A., López López, A., Baeza-Yates, R.: Flexible Comparison of Conceptual Graphs. Lecture Notes in Computer Science N 2113, Springer-Verlag, pp. 102-111 (2001)
78. Mosteller, F., Wallace, D.L.: Inference and Disputed Authorship: The Federalist. Reading, MA: Addison-Wesley Publishing Company (1964) (Reprinted: Stanford: Center for the Study of Language and Information (2008))

79. Padó, S., Lapata, M.: Dependency-based construction of semantic space models. Computational Linguistics, 33(2):161–199 (2007)
80. Padró, L., Collado, M., Reese, S., Lloberes, M., Castellón, I.: FreeLing 2.1: Five Years of Open-Source Language Processing Tools. In: Proceedings of 7th Language Resources and Evaluation Conference (LREC 2010), ELRA La Valletta, Malta (2010)
81. Padró, L., Stanilovsky, E.: FreeLing 3.0: Towards Wider Multilinguality. In: Proceedings of the Language Resources and Evaluation Conference (LREC 2012), ELRA, Turkey (2012)
82. Padro, L., Turmo, J.: TextServer: Cloud-based multilingual natural language processing. IEEE International Conference On Data Mining (2015)
83. Pentel, A. Effect of different feature types on age based classification of short texts. In: Proceedings of the 6th International Conference on Information, Intelligence, Systems and Applications, pp. 1–7 (2015)
84. Pichardo-Lagunas, O., Sidorov, G., Cruz-Cortés, N., Gelbukh, A.: Detección automática de primitivas semánticas en diccionarios explicativos con algoritmos bioinspirados. Onomazein, 28 (2013)
85. Posadas-Durán, J.-P., Gómez-Adorno, H., Sidorov, G., Batyrshin, I., Pinto, D., Chanona-Hernandez, L.: Application of the distributed document representation in the authorship attribution task for small corpora. Soft Computing, Vol. 21. No. 3, pp. 627–639 (2016)
86. Qian, T., Liu, B., Chen, L., Peng, Z.: Tritraining for authorship attribution with limited training data. In: Proceeding of the 52nd Annual Meeting of the Association for Computational Linguistics, pp. 345–351 (2014)
87. Reyes, J.A., Montes, A., González, J.G., Pinto, D.E.: Clasificación de roles semánticos usando características sintácticas, semánticas y contextuales. Computación y sistemas, 17(2): 263–272 (2013)
88. Ritter, A., Mausam, Etzioni, O.: A latent Dirichlet allocation method for selectional preferences. In: ACL, pp 424–434 (2010)
89. Sagae, K., Gordon, A.: Clustering words by syntactic similarity improves dependency parsing of predicate-argument structures. In IWPT, pp. 192–201 (2009)
90. Sapkota, U., Solorio, T., Montes-y-Gómez, M., Bethard, S., Rosso, P.: Cross-topic authorship attribution: Will out-of-topic data help? In: Proceedings of the 25th International Conference on Computational Linguistics, pp. 1228–1237 (2014)
91. Sapkota, U., Bethard, S., Montes-y-Gómez, M., Solorio, T. Not all character n-grams are created equal: A study in authorship attribution. In: Proceedings of the 2015 Annual Conference of the North American Chapter of the ACL: Human Language Technologies, pp. 93–102 (2015)
92. Sidorov, G., Ibarra Romero, M., Markov, I., Guzman-Cabrera, R., Chanona-Hernández, L., Velásquez, F.: Detección automática de similitud entre programas del lenguaje de programación Karel basada en técnicas de procesamiento de lenguaje natural. Computación y Sistemas, Vol. 20, No. 2, pp. 279–288 (2016)
93. Sidorov, G., Velasquez, F., Stamatatos, E., Gelbukh, A., Chanona-Hernández, L.: Syntactic Dependency-based N-grams as Classification Features. LNAI, 7630, pp. 1–11 (2012)
94. Sidorov, G., Velasquez, F., Stamatatos, E., Gelbukh, A., Chanona-Hernández, L.: Syntactic Dependency-Based N-grams: More Evidence of Usefulness in Classification. LNCS, 7816 (Proc. of CICLing), pp. 13–24 (2013)
95. Sidorov, G., Velasquez, F., Stamatatos, E., Gelbukh, A., Chanona-Hernández, L.: Syntactic N-grams as Machine Learning Features for Natural Language Processing. Expert Systems with Applications, 41(3): 853–860 (2014)
96. Sidorov, G.: N-gramas sintácticos y su uso en la lingüística computacional. Vectores de investigación, 6(6): 1–15 (2013)
97. Sidorov, G.: Non-continuous syntactic n-grams. Polibits, 48: 67–75 (2013)
98. Sidorov, G.: Syntactic Dependency Based N-grams in Rule Based Automatic English as Second Language Grammar Correction. International Journal of Computational Linguistics and Applications, 4(2): 169–188 (2013)

99. Sidorov, G.: Automatic Authorship Attribution Using Syllables as Classification Features. Rhema, Vol. 1, pp. 62–81 (2018)
100. Sierra, G., Alarcón, R.: Recurrent patterns in definitory context. In: Proc. CICLing-2002, Computational Linguistics and Intelligent Text Processing. Lecture Notes in Computer Science N 2276, Springer-Verlag, pp. 438–440 (2002)
101. Sierra, G., McNaught, J.: Natural Language System for Terminological Information Retrieval. Lecture Notes in Computer Science, N 2588, Springer, pp. 543–554 (2003)
102. Stamatatos, E.: A survey of modern authorship attribution methods. Journal of the American Society for information Science and Technology 60(3): 538–556 (2009)
103. Stamatatos, E.: On the robustness of authorship attribution based on character n-gram features. Journal of Law & Policy, Vol. 21, pp. 427–439 (2013)
104. Stamatatos, E., Daelemans, W., Verhoeven, B., Stein, B., Potthast, M., Juola, P., Sánchez-Pérez, M.A., Barrón-Cedeño, A.: Overview of the author identification task at PAN 2014. Working Notes of CLEF 2014 - Conference and Labs of the Evaluation forum, pp. 877–897 (2014)
105. Stamatatos, E., Daelemans, W., Verhoeven, B., Juola, P., López-López, A., Potthast, M., Stein, B.: Overview of the author identification task at PAN 2015. Working Notes of CLEF 2015 - Conference and Labs of the Evaluation forum (2015)
106. Stamatatos, E., Kokkinakis, G., Fakotakis, N.: Automatic text categorization in terms of genre and author. Computational Linguistics, Vol. 26, No. 4, pp. 471–495 (2000)
107. Van Halteren, H.: Linguistic profiling for author recognition and verification. In: Proceedings of the 42nd Annual Meeting on Association for Computational Linguistics (2004)
108. Wu, F., Weld, D.: Open information extraction using Wikipedia. In: ACL, pp. 118–127 (2010)

Printed in the United States
By Bookmasters